THE LIBRARY
ST. MARY'S COLLEGE OF MARYLAND
ST. MARY'S CITY, MARYLAND 20686

BROKEN BARS

BROKEN

UNIVERSITY OF NEW MEXICO PRESS
ALBUQUERQUE

BARS

KAY S. GARCIA

New Perspectives from Mexican Women Writers

©1994 by the University of New Mexico Press
All rights reserved.
First Edition

Library of Congress Cataloging in Publication Data

García, Kay S., 1951–
  Broken bars: new perspectives from
Mexican women writers / Kay S. García.—
1st ed.
    p. cm.
  Includes bibliographical references and
index.
  ISBN 0-8263-1512-7 (pbk.)
  1. Mexican literature—Women authors—
History and criticism.
2. Mexican literature—20th century—
History and criticism.
3. Authors, Mexican—20th
century-Interviews. 4. Women in literature.
  I. Title.
PQ7133.G37   1994
860.9′9287′0972–dc20
93-27814
CIP

Designed by Linda M. Tratechaud

To Bill and Verona García

TABLE OF CONTENTS

Preface *XI*
General Introduction *1*

PART I: ELENA PONIATOWSKA
Chapter One: Introduction *10*
Chapter Two: Interview *19*
Chapter Three: Challenging the Official Story:
Elena Poniatowska's *Massacre in Mexico* and *Nada, nadie*
(nothing, nobody) *33*

PART II: ANGELES MASTRETTA
Chapter Four: Introduction *63*
Chapter Five: Interview *71*
Chapter Six: Fidelity, Credibility, and Duplicity in
Angeles Mastretta's *Mexican Bolero* *89*

PART III: SILVIA MOLINA
Chapter Seven: Introduction *107*
Chapter Eight: Interview *113*
Chapter Nine: History and Herstory: Silvia Molina's
La familia vino del norte (the family came from the north)
and *Imagen de Héctor* (image of Hector) *131*

PART IV: BRIANDA DOMECQ

Chapter Ten: Introduction   *157*

Chapter Eleven: Interview   *165*

Chapter Twelve: Magic and Play in Brianda Domecq's *La insólita historia de la Santa de Cabora* (the unusual story of the saint from Cabora) and *Once días . . . y algo más* (eleven days . . . and even more)   *187*

Conclusion   *205*

Works Cited   *215*

Select Bibliography   *221*

ACKNOWLEDGMENTS

I AM GRATEFUL TO ALL THE FRIENDS AND COLLEAGUES WHO HELPED me with this manuscript, particularly: Brenda McCullough; Joseph Krause; Dianne Hart; Ray Verzasconi; Berta Aguilar, my Research Assistant; Pete Hale; E. Doris Tilles, Interlibrary Loan Librarian; and William Beezley.

I have to give special mention to Andrea Otañez, David LaFrance, and Barbara Guth for their careful editing and comments on the entire manuscript.

I am indebted to the following institutions for research and travel grants, and release time for writing the manuscript: Oregon Committee for the Humanities; OSU College of Liberal Arts; OSU Research Council; The Center for the Humanities, OSU; Women Faculty Development fund, OSU; Library Travel Grant, OSU.

Wise women can no longer be allowed as exceptions, eccentrics or witches, possessed of extra-human insight when they are possessed of any insight at all. Their rewriting of the human adventure is part of a necessary rewriting of history and of the future, which they will share with men. A politics which concerns itself with the future of the human race will need to refuse the blandishments of single or simple theories or solutions. It could do worse than begin from new readings of what women have said and written about a world organised to exclude them.

JANE MILLER,
WOMEN WRITING ABOUT MEN

PREFACE

One day in Madison, Wisconsin, I was walking behind my good friend Becky as she carried her sleeping daughter, and I noticed that her shoulders were exactly as narrow and fragile as mine. Becky had escaped from the island of St. Thomas and a former husband who had almost strangled her, and she was now a single parent working her way through law school. I had returned to graduate school with an infant and a toddler, and now I was working on my Ph.D. while teaching two classes per term and struggling with single parenthood. The sight of Becky's shoulders was a great comfort to me. If she could carry so much weight on them, then so could I. Even though my spirit was often daunted, I did manage to earn my doctorate, and at the present time I have a very satisfying job teaching Spanish composition and Latin American literature at Oregon State University.

What I hope to offer to the reader is my own set of fragile shoulders: here they are, measure yours by them, and see what you can do. I hope to inspire the reader with my story—particularly my involvement with the Mexican women writers presented here—as well as the stories of these four authors who have overcome incredible odds to become quite successful at their chosen profession.

In Mexico, the windows in many homes have iron bars on them, which serve as protection from intruders but also as symbolic enclosure for the women of the family. Bars can be found on the homes of people from all economic classes, in big cities as well as in small towns and rural areas. They symbolize the patriarch's power to control and contain the women of his family, the husband's right to demand undivided devotion, the brother's right to reject his sister's boyfriend, and the son's right to reproach his mother for stepping out of line. The authors presented in this book have figuratively broken the window bars

PREFACE

so that they can see out; I would also like to break the window bars so that the reader can see in, so the reader can know the intimate thoughts and experiences of these writers, how they have become interwoven with their texts, and the personal and social contexts that have shaped these thoughts and experiences.

To all of these ambitions, I add another goal: to create a text that is not only useful as a commentary on certain literary works but also can be enjoyed as a text in its own right. Although this has long been my intention, I found this concept beautifully expressed in an article by Janet Gold (1990), who points out the necessity to feel certain texts rather than just analyze them. I have tried to combine a finely tuned intuition with careful analysis and research in order to offer multiple perspectives on these authors and their works. In addition, I have drawn upon vital experiences—including my seven years teaching adults and raising children in Mexico, as part of a Mexican family and community—in order to understand these writers and their protagonists. In each woman I have found a portion of myself and it is my hope that the reader will make similar discoveries.

GENERAL
INTRODUCTION

Women will starve in silence
until new stories are created
which confer on them
the power of naming themselves.

Sandra Gilbert and Susan Gubar,
The Mad Woman in the Attic

IF THE WOMEN OF THE WORLD WERE NOT PROVIDED WITH PHYSIcal sustenance—if their bodies were not being fed—there would be a tremendous outcry, because everyone would realize the danger to the human race if all females were to perish. Without overlooking the very real problem of physical hunger in the world, I would like to call attention to a kind of deprivation that is more insidious because it is less recognized: the starvation of women's imagination.

Traditionally, women's roles in literature have been limited to those of madonna or whore; the plot lines find them choosing between marriage or death.[1] Only in the twentieth century have writers such as Doris Lessing and Barbara Kingsolver dared to present protagonists who forge their own destiny. The same thing is happening in Mexico, but positive role models are still difficult to find. In Mexican literature there are two dominant female archetypes that correspond roughly to the traditional madonna/whore split: the Virgin of Guadalupe, who represents the pure, virtuous woman; and the Malinche, who symbolizes the treacherous, loose woman.[2] Although some female characters are breaking away from these archetypes, negative role models abound: Elena Garro's protagonists escape into fantasy, or triumph only after death; Amparo Dávila's characters retreat into insanity;

---

[1]*Rachel Blau DuPlessis has analyzed the marriage-or-death dilemma of nineteenth-century heroines, and shown how some twentieth-century writers have created new choices for their protagonists, in her book* Writing Beyond the Ending.

[2]*For a more complete analysis of these two types, see Luis Leal's article "Female Archetypes in Mexican Literature," in* Women in Hispanic Literature: Icons and Fallen Idols *(Berkeley: U of California P, 1983), 227–42. Also see Sandra Messinger Cypess's book* La Malinche in Mexican Literature *(Austin: U of Texas P, 1991).*

GENERAL INTRODUCTION

Rosario Castellano's characters are caught in loveless marriages or other restrictive situations; Sara Sefchovich's protagonists lose themselves in prostitution or endless, meaningless travels.³ The female characters of most contemporary Mexican women writers follow the same patterns. Now and then a glimmer of autonomy will appear in fiction—notably in stories by Ethel Krause, Inés Arredondo, and María Luisa Mendoza—but book-length depictions of strong Mexican women who shape their own lives are few indeed.

Modern writers need to inscribe alternate lives upon the female imagination, as Carolyn Heilbrun pointed out in her book *Writing a Woman's Life*. Women need to read about other possibilities, about successful women who do not subordinate their lives to a man's life. New solutions that involve solitary quests or pursuits supported by nontraditional partners need to be found. In order for this to happen, Heilbrun suggests, women need to speak profoundly and truthfully to one another. We need to share our experiences, to tell our lives as they really are, and to shape them in new ways. Writers can facilitate this process by creating female heroes rather than heroines.⁴ This has been done to different degrees by the four authors I have chosen to present in this book: Elena Poniatowska, Angeles Mastretta, Silvia Molina, and Brianda Domecq.

Along with new ways of writing, there must be new ways of reading, and for inspiration I turn to Janet Gold, who has said, "If one listens to the text rather than talking at it, it becomes a conversation among women seeking to define and refine the tools of narrative" (196). I would like to further this conversation among women, relying on intuition and self-recognition to reach the inner space described by Gold:

> It is this locus, this interior reservoir, both tangible and
> ephemeral, that as a woman reading a woman I recognize. As

---

³*It is not my intention to give a complete overview of Mexican women writers, as that has already been done by Jean Franco, in* Plotting Women, *and by Martha Robles, in* La sombra fugitiva *(the furtive shadow).*
⁴*Female hero is an expression explained by Carolyn Heilbrun in* Toward a Recognition of Androgyny. *Briefly, it refers to a woman who shapes her own life rather than waiting around for a Prince Charming to save her from having to make any decisions.*

the flesh of its discourse enfolds me I find myself in a deep familiar place. My center communicates with the center transformed of these texts and my reading (dialogue) becomes a (re)-creation of myself. The woman center proves to be not empty or passively waiting to be filled, but rather the generator of images, the teller of tales, and a source of strength, as well as the space within which women may spend time with themselves. (202)

The stories women tell are different from stories men tell, but it is not simply a question of feminine imagery or emotional involvement in the narrative. Granted, sometimes women do use proportionately more images, or they emphasize feelings more frequently, but these qualities are not the exclusive property of female writers. What women writers can contribute—and men can only imitate—is the point of view of a woman, derived from the personal experience that only a woman can have. With increasing frequency, women writers are telling the other side of the story, and as Molly Hite has affirmed, "the act of telling the other side alters the story irrevocably" (89).

One of the narrative tools that women have employed in order to tell the other side of the story is *counter-discourse,* a literary tactic discussed by Richard Terdiman in his *Discourse/Counter-Discourse.* According to Terdiman, dominant discourse consists of "a culture's determined and determining structures of representation and practice" (12). It shapes people's perceptions of themselves and of society, and, as Terdiman points out, "such practices impose their violence not only upon things, but upon us too" (15). Terdiman examines certain strains of dominant discourse in nineteenth-century European literature and then presents "the principal discursive systems by which writers and artists sought to project an alternative, liberating *newness* against the absorptive capacity of those established discourses" (13). He calls these liberating narratives *counter-discourse.* I have borrowed Terdiman's term and adapted it to the realities of twentieth-century Mexico. I use *counter-discourse* to refer to the narrative techniques authors employ in order to contradict the dominant discourse (which I also refer to as the *official discourse,* because much of it is generated

GENERAL INTRODUCTION

by the Mexican government or by historians sanctioned by the government). Seeing counter-discourse as principally a negation of the official story, I use the term *alternative discourse* to refer to a more positive narration that deviates from the official discourse by creating a personal or collective story that affirms the vitality and creativity of the narrators and protagonists. All four of the authors presented here use both counter- and alternative discourse, to different degrees and with diverse purposes.

One of the obvious weapons in the literary battle against dominant discourse is intertextuality, which in general terms means the relationship of a text to other, preexisting texts. Intertextuality is explicit if the original texts are quoted, and implicit if there are vague references to texts and no mention of authors or titles. Intertextuality may be either supportive or subversive of the original meaning of the excerpt, but in either case the previous text undergoes a semantic transformation.[5] In *La noche de Tlatelolco* (*Massacre in Mexico*) and *Nada, nadie: Las voces del temblor* (nothing, nobody: voices from the earthquake),[6] Elena Poniatowska uses explicit intertextuality to undermine the credibility of the official government rhetoric. Angeles Mastretta's *Arráncame la vida* (*Mexican Bolero*) has an implicit intertextual relationship with the official accounts of the life of a powerful Mexican politician. Silvia Molina uses implicit and explicit intertextuality with texts that are both internal and external to her fictional space, as she reshapes the image of herself and her family members in *La familia vino del norte* (the family came from the north) and *Imagen de Héctor* (image of Hector). The official image of a controversial folk healer is transformed by means of intertextuality in Brianda Domecq's *La insólita historia de la Santa de Cabora* (the unusual story of the saint from Cabora).

---

[5] *These concepts are taken from Laurent Jenny's article, "The strategy of form" (see Works Cited).*

[6] *In this book, works that have been translated into English will have the Spanish title followed by the English title in italics and in parentheses. After several such identifications, the English title will be used. Works that have not been translated into English will have the Spanish title followed by an English translation in parentheses, but without italics or capital letters. The title will be translated the first time it is mentioned in each chapter.*

GENERAL INTRODUCTION

In addition to similar literary techniques, these authors' works have several major themes in common: the dilemma of the modern woman, political corruption in Mexico, and a search for personal and national identity. In spite of the difference in their ages—Molina and Mastretta are in their mid-forties, Domecq is about fifty, and Poniatowska is about sixty—they are all actively engaged in writing at the present time, and they have all contributed to the tremendous surge in literature by Mexican women that has occurred in the last fifteen years. All four women are economically secure, although in order to earn a living they have had to work in related fields such as journalism, editing, and translating. Even though they come from the upper middle class, they have given voice to the concerns of the indigent and indigenous people of Mexico. They all have had to struggle to combine the duties of wife, mother, and writer.

These authors have a deeply felt commitment to their writing: Poniatowska was so involved in the tragedy of *Nada, nadie,* the story of the 1985 earthquake that devastated Mexico City, that she became ill and it took her a long time to recover. Mastretta has pushed herself so hard—as she juggles publicity tours, mothering two young children, journalism, and writing her next novel—that the second time I visited her (in 1992), I found her totally exhausted and suffering from an ulcer. Molina's powers of organization and time management have enabled her to teach literature at the national university, direct a publishing house, spend time with her family, and continue to produce short stories and novels. Domecq was so involved in the subject of her second novel that it dominated her life for seventeen years, becoming an obsession that she transformed into spiritual possession in her narrative.

Works by all of these authors have been widely reviewed, and in general the reviews have been very positive. Their books are used in literature classes at prestigious universities such as the National Autonomous University of Mexico (UNAM), the Colegio de México (college of Mexico), and the University of the Americas in Puebla. All of them have received recognition in Mexico, and Poniatowska and Mastretta also have had considerable success in the United States and Europe. Molina and Domecq

GENERAL INTRODUCTION

should soon receive more attention from outside Mexico, as the English translation of Molina's first novel has recently been released and the translation of Domecq's first novel has just been completed.

The most significant contribution these four authors have made to Mexican literature has been their presentation of emancipatory alternatives for women. They have created literary characters who break away from society's dictums and shape their own lives. Poniatowska has also presented real women who had important roles in the rescue efforts after the earthquake: housewives who coordinated the delivery of food and supplies, volunteers who participated in the excavations, seamstresses who organized to improve living and working conditions for themselves. Each of these authors is also a role model in her own right, living proof that women can and do combine family and professional obligations, but with difficulty. The struggles and sacrifices of these writers should not be glossed over; it is not my intention to contribute to the "superwoman" myth. Rather, I would like to nourish women's imaginations, offering new and liberating possibilities by showing counter- and alternative discourse at work in women's texts and in women's lives. For that reason I have included a personal introduction to each author (in which I refer to each one by her first name, because I am talking about her as a person, not just a writer). I have also included an interview with each author, so the reader can witness for himself/herself the complicated relationship between these writers and their texts. Not only do their lives shape their texts, but their texts shape their lives. To get to the deepest meaning of their work it is necessary to enter their lives. The final chapter in each part is an analysis of one or two works that draws upon literary theory and analytical terms as well as on the information revealed in the interviews and my own intuition as a reader and a writer. Although I arrive at some conclusions, the reader of this book is invited to make his/her own identifications and extrapolations, contributing to the further generation of meaning.

PART I
ELENA PONIATOWSKA

Chapter One
Introduction

It is preferable to die than to not
do things with passion.

ELENA PONIATOWSKA

ELENA LETS ME IN TO HER COZY HOME IN CHIMALISTÁC, MEXICO City, where she has allowed so many others to enter: student protesters, striking workers, laid-off seamstresses, grieving mothers, witnesses of tragedy. I feel privileged to be included in their number. Elena finds her own sorrow—and strength—in all of these people. She is a beautiful woman, in the deepest and truest meaning, with a sense of sturdiness in spite of her slight stature. Her thick blond hair is laden with gray, and her eyes, heavily underlined by her own suffering and that of others, reveal compassion and bravery. Her courage to publish criticism of the government is remarkable, considering the fate of so many journalists in Mexico: sixty Mexican journalists were killed at work between 1970 and 1990, and during those same years another 366 reporters were attacked while on the job (Barry 246).

Elena takes me through her small living room, which is overflowing with books, photographs of friends and family, and souvenirs from diverse areas of the world. As she walks, everything she passes reflects her; she is connected to the tiles on the floor, the white plaster on the walls, the heavy woven curtains; she belongs here. She takes me up to her tiny office, where the two of us barely fit between a computer and a large bookshelf. Elena takes me in and sees me, she knows me. She has an extraordinary capacity to connect to people, to feel their emotions, to meet them and within minutes be listening to their innermost secrets. Elena explains her connection to the universe with these words:

> I have always walked. I think as I stroll along: How much of me there is in these faces that don't know me and that I don't know, how much of me in the subway, in the steps that pile up, . . . how much of me in the rain that forms puddles on the pavement, . . . how much of me in the Colonia del Valle-

ELENA PONIATOWSKA

Coyoacán buses that rush along until they crash and form part of the cosmos. (Poniatowska 1991, 91)

When Elena is portrayed in the newspapers, she is often drawn with angel's wings and an enormous smile. While talking to me, that smile is easy, it comes often and from deep within her. Elena explains the source of that smile:

> I would like to return to earth because I love life. I would like to gaze, even from afar, on the grandchildren of my grandchildren and on everyone's grandchildren, to see the trees, . . . the city square of the Zócalo, . . . the sea on the coast of Oaxaca, the turtles that Francisco Toledo paints, his grasshoppers, the rabbit that laughs, and the fox that pokes fun at us all. (Poniatowska 1991, 89)

Elena's Spanish is sometimes laced with a slight French accent, and she punctuates her sentences with the question "no?" which could be translated "isn't that right?" or "don't you think so?" She is humble and unassuming, and it is hard for me to believe that she was referred to as *la princesa* at the newspaper office where she started working at the age of twenty. Perhaps they were referring to her noble ancestors: she is descended from Stanislaus Augustus Poniatowski, the last king of Poland before the partitioning of that country in 1795 (Pedén 47). According to Elena, Stanislaus loved Catherine the Great, who made him king of Poland in order to get rid of him. He wrote her passionate letters: "I don't want to be king, I want to be in your bed" (Poniatowska 1991, 94). After the partitioning of Poland, the Poniatowskis were exiled to France, where they lived for generations. Elena's father was born in France, where he became a war hero. Elena remembers him as a distant man, who only expressed his feelings on the piano.

Elena's mother was the daughter of a Mexican landowner who lost his hacienda in the Mexican Revolution. Her mother's family traveled throughout Europe, never seeming to belong anywhere. Sometime during these travels, her parents met and settled briefly in France, where Elena was born in 1933. During the Second World War, Elena's father was at the front, and her mother

INTRODUCTION

drove an ambulance until she got into trouble for loading a wounded burro into her vehicle. When Elena was nine years old, she moved to Mexico with her mother and her sister; her father joined them after the war.

From bustling France, Elena arrived on the vast desert plains of Mexico, and she wanted desperately to belong to this rugged country. Her mother, whom Elena describes as ethereal and elusive, spoke French at home. Elena learned Spanish and much about Mexican life from the maids, following them around and asking endless questions. This period of Elena's life is described in her autobiographical novel *La "Flor de Lis"* (the "fleur-de-lis").

Elena attended French and English schools in Mexico, and the Sacred Heart Convent in Philadelphia, where her formal schooling ended. After returning to Mexico, she started writing newspaper articles and interviews for the cultural supplement of the Mexico City newspaper *Novedades* (news), and she was so successful that soon she was publishing an interview a day, including conversations with celebrities such as Diego Rivera, Luis Buñuel, Jorge Luis Borges, and Gabriel García Márquez. She also directed cultural programs for radio and television, and published poems, short stories, essays, chronicles, and novels. She traveled to Cuba, Brazil, Venezuela, the United States, Europe, Cuba, Czechoslovakia, and Vietnam. All this she managed to do while being married to the astronomer Guillermo Haro, and having three children, although it was not easy. "For me it is difficult to be a housewife and especially to feel the responsibility of the children," she explains (Miller 305, my translation).

Elena and I are setting up our chairs, placing the tape recorder between us, and she is called to the phone by her daughter. When she comes back, her son Felipe comes in to use the computer, and Elena squeezes over to allow him to sit down. Felipe, who was only a few weeks old when his mother started interviewing survivors of the massacre of 1968,[1] seems irritated by my presence. I am just one more person that his mother is interviewing.

---

[1] On 2 October 1968, the Mexican government ordered troops to ambush and fire upon the student demonstrators in the plaza of Tlatelolco. Several hundred were killed, and thousands were wounded or arrested.

ELENA PONIATOWSKA

As I try to make more room for him, my left arm is pressed against a bookshelf where Elena's own works are scattered among texts from all over the world. Elena's books have been translated into English, French, German, Italian, Polish, and Czechoslovakian. She was awarded the National Journalism Prize in 1978, and the Mazatlán Literary Prize for her 1969 novel *Hasta no verte, Jesús mío* (here's to you, Jesus). She rejected the prestigious Villaurrutia Prize, which was awarded to her for *La noche de Tlatelolco* (translated as *Massacre in Mexico*), asking President Luis Echeverría in an open letter if someone was going to give a prize to all those killed in 1968. She was also named the Mexican Woman of the Year and given a prize called the Coatlicue by the magazine *Debate Feminista* (feminist debate) in 1990, in honor of her work in support of women writers.

Unlike many Mexican writers who claim not to be feminists, Elena is open about her affiliations: "It would be absurd to say that I am not a feminist. I am completely on the side of women, I want women to progress" (Miller 320, my translation). Elena has written prologues for women's works, she presents their books, and she has given workshops for and about women writers, at both the University of California–Davis and the National Autonomous University of Mexico. Although she has been a mentor to many women writers, the only female author that she mentions as someone who has nourished her writing is Rosario Castellanos.[2] She also mentions Juan Rulfo, Carlos Fuentes, José Agustín, Juan José Arreola, and Octavio Paz.

Elena writes in order to relate to other people; what she is too timid to say out loud, she writes (Miller 303). She refers to her characteristic manner of narrating as "testimonial literature," which combines methods of oral testimony with elements of history, fiction writing, and new journalism. She grapples with doubts about her writing, and with a pervasive sense of guilt that underlies much of her reporting. She is very aware of the contrast between her own comfortable existence and that of the people

---

[2]*Rosario Castellanos (1925–74) was a Mexican author well known for her indigenist novels such as* Oficio de tinieblas *(profession of darkness) and for her poetry, collected in* Poesía no eres tú *(poetry you are not).*

INTRODUCTION

she interviews. At the same time that her texts document the misery and exploitation of the country's poor people, they also constitute an eloquent testimony of the problematic process of writing literature based on oral history (Steele 1987, 211).

In the summer of 1968, Elena followed the student demonstrations with trepidation, unable to attend because she was expecting a baby. On 3 October, three women came to her home and told her that the army and police had massacred many men, women, and children in the plaza of Tlatelolco in Mexico City. Elena thought they were hysterical, so the next day she went to the plaza to see for herself. There she saw all the bullet holes on the walls, the blood still not washed away, the army still there; many people had abandoned their homes around the plaza, and personal items were scattered on the ground. She started listening to the stories of those who wanted to talk, and the result was her book *La noche de Tlatelolco,* which is now in its forty-ninth printing.

Ten years later she published *Fuerte es el silencio* (strong is the silence), a collection of essays, one of which is an afterword about the massacre. Other essays in this book include a description of the lives of the poorest people in Mexico City, a diary of a hunger strike by women whose sons have disappeared in the Mexican jail system, and the story of a grassroots organization that established a colony for homeless people. Then in 1985 an earthquake hit Mexico City, and Elena served once again as the voice of the people. First she participated in the rescue work, carrying buckets of debris from the ruins and helping at the shelters, but then she received a message from the journalist Carlos Monsiváis: "What is the best chronicler of Mexico doing sitting in her home? . . . Start writing" (Steele 1989, 101). Elena published articles in the newspapers for fifty days, first in *Novedades* and then in *La Jornada* (the workday), until she was told that they were too depressing to publish. Suspecting that the government had pressured the newspapers to stop publishing her articles, she began gathering them into a book. Students enrolled in her literary workshop helped with the rescue effort also, and then contributed articles and testimony to Elena's book. She spoke with everybody that she could, without taping the stories, but rather writing them down at night by memory. She couldn't just write, however—she would go find her interviewees a wheelchair, some food, or medicine—she just couldn't isolate herself from the problems she was recording (Steele 1989, 104). When she was so exhausted that she couldn't work on the manuscript any longer, she turned it over to her publisher, and *Nada, nadie: Las voces del temblor* (nothing, nobody: voices from the earthquake) was born.

In addition to the works already mentioned, Elena has published the following collections of her interviews: *Palabras cruzadas* (crossword); *Domingo 7* (Sunday the seventh), in which she interviews the 1982 presidential candidates; and *Todo México* (all of Mexico). She has also published a collection of literary essays, *Ay vida, no me mereces* (oh, life, you don't deserve me), and the story of a woman with cerebral palsy who manages to educate herself and to adopt a child, *Gaby Brimmer*. In tribute to her adopted homeland, she has published *El último guajolote* (the last turkey), about disappearing Mexican traditions; *Todo empezó en domingo* (everything started on Sunday), about the celebrations of the poor; and *La casa en la tierra* (the house on the earth) about the homes of poor people in the country.

Elena's fiction usually portrays strong female characters. She has published two collections of short stories: *Lilus Kikus* (the name of a young girl) and *De noche vienes* (you come by night), many of which have been translated into English and published in anthologies and literary journals. However, she has received the most recognition for her novel *Hasta no verte, Jesús mío,* which is a long monologue by the protagonist, an impoverished woman who had an active role in the Mexican Revolution. Another work of hers that has received a lot of attention is *Querido Diego, te abraza Quiela* (Dear Diego, Affectionately, Quiela), which may be published in English with the title *Dear Diego*. This is an epistolary novel, a collection of fictional letters that the Russian painter Angelina Beloff wrote to Diego Rivera after living with him in Paris for ten years and having his son. When Diego returned to his native country, he promised to send money to Angelina so that she could join him. He never sent any money, and when she finally traveled to Mexico and spoke to Diego on the street, he passed by without recognizing her. Angelina did not try to con-

INTRODUCTION

tact him after that humiliation. This anecdote inspired Elena to write the novel, to illustrate the contrasting public and private images of a famous man.

Elena and I are ready now, and Felipe grudgingly interrupts his work on the computer to leave us alone. The tape recorder is set up between us, the microphone is turned on, and the interview begins.

Chapter Two

Interview
Elena Poniatowska

ELENA PONIATOWSKA

KG: Your novel about Tina Modotti, called *Tinísima* (very, very Tina; or Tina the Great) is already out, am I right?[1]

EP: Yes, it came out in September 1992. There will also be a book of chronicles and essays, called *Luz y luna las lunitas* (light and moon, the little moons), with Ediciones Era. That's what I would like to publish next, but sometimes I feel that I don't have enough strength to handle so many things that I am asked to do, even though curiosity is killing me. I always think that maybe I am missing something very important if I don't do a certain thing.

KG: You also have to dedicate time to your family, isn't that so?

EP: Of course, that too, one has to live and to spend time with the family.

KG: That's how it is for many of us [women], our time is very limited. I would like to know more about your other projects, but first I would like to ask you about *Massacre in Mexico* and *Nada, nadie* (nothing, nobody). Do you feel the connection between these two books?

EP: Yes, but I also feel that there is a strong connection with another book of mine, which is called *Fuerte es el silencio* (strong is the silence), and all three have something in common, but in regard to *Massacre in Mexico* and *Nada, nadie*, one is about a massacre and the other is about an earthquake. One describes a natural phenomenon, an earthquake, but in regard to the very, very slow reaction of the government, and in the case of *Massacre in Mexico* I speak about the very rapid reaction of the government that kills the students. And then *Fuerte es el silencio* retrieves again the theme of *Massacre in Mexico* because it is about the student movement, also.

KG: The massacre of 1968 is still having repercussions in present-day Mexico, right? In fact, in *Nada, nadie* several people remember 1968 because [the earthquake] was so catastrophic, especially in the plaza of Tlatelolco.

EP: Yes, I believe that they were both catastrophes, like you say, and what caught my attention was finding the same people

---

[1] *This interview is a compilation of conversations that I had with Elena Poniatowska in December of 1989 and in August of 1992.*

INTERVIEW

in 1985 that I had seen in 1968. That means that these people kept alive their ideals, their social commitment, their desire to help others, and the same social conscience that they had in '68, and that impressed me very much, it had a big impact on me.

KG: Do you believe that there is a curse on the plaza of Tlatelolco?

EP: No, I don't believe that at all, I believe that the plaza of Tlatelolco is just like any other public square in the world, don't you think so?

KG: So you think it's just a coincidence that these catastrophes happened in the same place?

EP: Yes. I don't believe in things like witchcraft and curses.

KG: Have you read the book by Carlos Martínez?

EP: Which book?

KG: A book called *Tres instantáneas* (three snapshots); it is about three instances of violence in the plaza of Tlatelolco. It begins with the time the Aztecs defeated the Tlatelolcas in that square in 1473, and then the second instance is when the Spaniards conquered the Aztecs in 1521.

EP: And the third is the massacre [of 1968]?

KG: Yes, and then there's also the disaster of 1985.

EP: Even so, I don't believe that the poor plaza is cursed.

KG: So much the better for those who still live there.

EP: Of course.

KG: Your own narrative voice is more noticeable in *Nada, nadie* than in *Massacre in Mexico*. Is this due to the material, or to the fact that you have matured as a chronicler?

EP: No, I think that I hardly appear in *Nada, nadie,* except in the episode when I went to the Museum of Anthropology and I saw the politicians and the president of the Republic, but generally I do not appear.

KG: Once in a while it seems like it is your opinion that is being offered.

EP: Yes, once in a while. It is a frightful book. I believe that it is not polished, that it doesn't all fit together. I started working on the first pages in order to transform them into a book and then I couldn't do it any longer, the material was so difficult to manage and so upsetting that I took it to the publisher and I said if you want to make a book, here is the material, but it was like a block, I couldn't work on that book. I didn't have time to do it, but it was really a question of not having the strength to do it.

KG: Nevertheless the pieces of the narration, even though they are fragments, form a montage that has consistency and coherence.

EP: That's encouraging because I never thought that it was well done.

KG: You allow the reader to be active, to remember an incident that has already been described by a previous narrator. So the reader has to be very aware, and to make the connections, which is very typical of the narrative of the twentieth century. Carlos Fuentes writes like that; the reader has to work hard to understand his works.

EP: Well, you are encouraging me.

KG: I really liked *Nada, nadie*. I was wondering, how much of the book was yours? There are some segments that you identify as written by somebody else; did you write all the rest?

EP: All of it.

KG: Many times you are summarizing other people's words, or other people's stories, right?

EP: Yes, or what other people told me. But in general the whole book, everything that isn't signed by somebody else, I wrote myself.

KG: Can you tell me about the women that you interviewed for this book? What were they like?

EP: Well, I interviewed a lot of seamstresses, so many that I am going to write a whole book on them. Some of them stand out in my mind, like Evangelina Corona and many more, because of their bravery, their integrity, their intelligence, and many other things about them that caught my attention.

KG: Have you suffered negative consequences for your severe criticism of the Mexican government?

EP: Well, they've never given me an important position, I will never be a millionaire, never anything, but they have never put me in jail.

INTERVIEW

KG: And that's no little thing.
EP: That is a lot.
KG: At least they allow you to write and to publish.
EP: They allow me to write and to publish, and they have never done anything to me.
KG: I'm very glad of that.
EP: I am too. (Laughter)
KG: You could live anywhere in the world. Why do you stay in Mexico City?
EP: I've lived here since I was a girl, and it is a city I love, because I work here and I feel like I am a part of it.
KG: How can you stand to be the witness and chronicler of so much suffering and so much injustice?
EP: Well as you can see, I can't stand it, for example, with *Nada, nadie* I got sick and it took me a long time to recuperate. If there is a third tragedy here in Mexico, I won't be able to chronicle anything, it will have to be someone younger. I won't be able to get involved at all because I know that would be the end of me; no, it is too much already.
KG: The catastrophes weigh you down; they accumulate.
EP: Yes, and even if you recuperate, and try to forget, and even though time is a marvelous healer, when something happens again it opens the old wound that was still very tender, very rotten, or fragile, and then I can't [do any more].
KG: Yes, I understand. (pause) Well let's go on to another topic so we don't get too sad. In your article "La toma de la literatura" (taking literature by force), written in 1983, you complain that women allow themselves to be caught up by the rivalry over men, by running a home, and by paralyzing and stupidifying beauty—"*la belleza paralizadora y estupidizante*"—I love that phrase.
EP: The compulsion to be beautiful like in *Vogue*.
KG: Exactly. Do you believe that Mexican women writers have progressed much in the last ten years?
EP: I think so. There are some young writers who have a lot to offer. There are some poets—Silvia Tomasa Rivera, Kiyra Galván—who are much more free than the writers before them. There are other young writers like Carmen Boullosa and

Bárbara Jacobs who belong to the next generation after Angeles Mastretta and who have achieved much greater liberty than we have.

KG: Do you think that woman's voice in literature is different than the masculine voice? And how is it different, or what difference do you notice between a novel written by a woman and one written by a man?

EP: I think that we have great fortune in Mexico because we have a phenomenon which is still a phenomenon in the twentieth century even though it began in the seventeenth century, and that is Sor Juana Inés de la Cruz. She herself said: "If I am a woman, may nobody verify that fact." It's not that she denied being a woman, but what mattered to her above all was to write, and she wanted to express herself through writing. She is a unique case but I do believe that there is a difference between a book written by a woman and a book written by a man. I think that women always have more images, we are more emotional and a lot more sensitive. We have a degree of sensitivity which is much more developed, much more acute, than in men, but we have much less ability to synthesize and to organize. You have done some studies of Elena Garro's novels, and what you could say about her novels, with the exception of *Recollections of Things to Come,* which is excellent, is that they are not balanced. They are not analyzed, there is no synopsis in each part of the novel, there is no analysis, such as in this part I am going to say this, in the next part I am going to say that, I am going to write an exposition or a central part and a denouement or a climax or an anticlimax. Elena Garro mixes everything up and sometimes she mixes the tenses, she mixes the characters; it is a mixture of everything, there is no order or logic, not even a structural order, which a novel written by a man would have. Therefore I think that structurally we write differently and our themes are those that men sometimes wouldn't choose, in spite of Flaubert and his *Madame Bovary,* in spite of there being Mexican [male] writers who have written like women, but they have not created female characters who are worthwhile, who have forged ahead, who have been outstanding, there aren't any.

INTERVIEW

KG: We need more positive models, that's something that I am seeking also.
EP: Or at least models of women even if they aren't positive, but there aren't any, well, there's Malinche, and *La LLorona*,² but really you don't see women who are saying, "I'm going to do this," right?
KG: Yes, and we really need them.
EP: The few women who are in Latin American literature are very poorly presented, very evil, like the main character in Rómulo Gallegos' novel, *Doña Bárbara*.
KG: What advice would you give to North American women who are literary critics and literature professors? What would you suggest that we do, what should we write about?
EP: Look, I don't have any advice for the critics because I don't know about criticism, but I can tell you that if the Latin American women writers are known in the United States it is because of the departments of Spanish and Portuguese, or Romance Languages. It is the women professors who have worked to invite women writers that never before were invited by the men of those departments. Women writers have not even been recognized in Mexico, but they have been taken into account in the United States.
KG: You mentioned [in an earlier conversation] that one of your projects is a novel about a North American woman who falls in love with a Mexican man.
EP: Yes, this is a novel that I really want to write because it is something that I have seen here, and I think that I can feel it because I also was not born in Mexico. I want to write a love story. Besides, I have seen many North American girls who come here with a very open and innocent attitude. Since they come wearing their shorts and their miniskirts, one can see their democratic attitude, because in Mexico the social classes are completely differentiated and there is a way of treating

---

²*Malinche was Hernán Cortés's indigenous lover who betrayed her people by serving as his interpreter, thus helping him win allies among the indigenous enemies of the Aztecs and facilitating the Conquest. La Llorona is a mythical woman who some people claim they can hear at night as she weeps for her dead children.*

people according to the way they dress. The novel is really a confrontation of two cultures. It is about a girl who is very confident and who has an enormous degree of spontaneity which women in Mexico do not know, in the way that they dress and everything. They have a degree of freedom and in a certain way innocence and purity, which is not understood here, and it is interpreted in a bad way. Here a woman walks down the street in the center of town, wearing shorts or a short skirt and some tennis shoes or sandals—which they do quite naturally because it is hot here in Mexico—and the men act like a pack of wolves. Why? Because Mexican women don't do that here; so it is really a confrontation of two cultures.

This girl [the protagonist of my novel] is enchanted not only by the city and by the country, but also by the whole culture. And she discovers that the Mexican culture is much more rich than the North American culture, because of the pre-Columbian cultures which are being explored so extensively during that period—the novel will take place in the fifties or sixties—when a whole country is discovering itself, evaluating itself, great collections of pre-Columbian works are put in new museums, more and more searches are planned. All of that becomes an obsession, and for the girl, a passion. She doesn't realize to what degree she is put down, pushed aside, considered just a gringa, until after her great and generous love affair with both a man and his country, when she goes to a place called Temico and she is raped by a group of *campesinos* (men who work in the fields). This rape makes her aware of all of the other times that she has been violated in this country, all of the violence that has been done to her, including being ridiculed for her spontaneity. She had to deal with men competing with each other to "get" a gringa, and with the reputation that gringas have: they go to Acapulco and go out with the men who drive the boats, they get drunk on the beach and dance all night, that kind of thing.

The Mexican macho is always ready not only to dominate a woman, but also to squash her if he can; when he has squashed her and rubbed her into the floor, then he says, "Now you need me." Then he picks up that human garbage, that mop on

INTERVIEW

the floor, and then she is his woman who will wait on him, bring him coffee, take care of him and more or less take care of his children, because he has taken all of her blood, all of her will and desire to do something in life other than serve him and be his self-sacrificing little wife. Now that doesn't happen to women just because they are gringas, it happens to any woman in Mexico who wants to do more than be a self-sacrificing wife, because Mexican husbands in any field will not tolerate a woman who does more than that. It is a problem of competition, and of custom, and also because many women accept it. There are politicians who have wives who are content to be in charge of the house, and many rich people whose wives run the house and their only activities without their husbands are getting manicures, pedicures, and hairdos, buying dresses, playing cards, having a group of friends, that kind of life. There are many women who accept that life-style and don't try to do anything else.

KG: Your novel is going to be very complex, and interesting.

EP: Well I don't know how it's going to be because I haven't even started it yet, and before that I want to do another one. But I do want to be collecting information because I want to include a lot about the pre-Columbian world, of which I know very little.

KG: What is the other book that you want to write?

EP: It is a novel about a man who decides to be a scientist in a third-world country, and he manages to be a great scientist; he was recognized as an astronomer, and Mexico has contributed a lot to the field of astronomy. So it is the story of a man who decides that he will do science in Mexico at a time when there was no science in Mexico and it didn't matter to anybody. Mexico is always interested in "know how," all the North American technology, and they say that it is cheaper to import technology than to set up scientists with laboratories and equipment here. They say why do we want a nuclear reactor here, why do we want any apparatus, but it's not really a question of why do we want it, the truth is that there is no budget dedicated to science. In Latin America I think Argentina and Chile are more advanced in science, but not

Mexico, except in astronomy. I think that change is very interesting, especially in a country where everybody wants to be a lawyer and get into government and become corrupt and steal all that they can. If you go to the university, the schools that are full are law and medicine. Thanks to who-knows-what, there is finally some development of science.

Guillermo Haro, my husband who died five years ago [in 1987], was a scientist. So I want to write the story of a life, but it's not his life. It's not going to be like a biography, but rather like a novel. I want to start everything with a feeling of guilt. He feels guilty, and he does a series of things, because he believes that he killed a woman; he didn't kill her but his whole life he believes that he killed her.

KG: So it is another kind of confrontation.

EP: Yes, it is another kind of confrontation, and it is a novel that I would really like to write, before the other one, because the other one I need to think over more, I want to talk to [North American] women who have had experiences with Mexicans.

Now, I don't want to write an anti-Mexican novel, because obviously the rape could be perceived as totally anti-Mexican; they could say, "Why does the rape occur in Mexico, aren't there rapes in the United States?" I want to write it so that it's not anti-Mexican, so that it's a fair treatment.

KG: So in that novel you are also going to try to bring out some positive aspects of Mexico, aren't you? Not just the rape, but other things, too.

EP: Of course! Besides, in the first half of the novel the hero has to be Mexico, because the protagonist is dazzled by a culture she has never seen, the magic and everything. I think that Mexico is a fascinating country for someone who comes from another country.

KG: I think that if you emphasize that in the novel, it won't be an anti-Mexican novel.

EP: Of course. It is a very rich setting.

KG: Besides, you could emphasize the importance of the family, the way people treat each other, the human warmth that there is in Mexico.

INTERVIEW

EP: Yes, there is a lot of human warmth here, and the people can be very receptive, very affectionate.
KG: Do you have any other projects?
EP: I have a prologue for a book [already in print] by Ana Gutiérrez called *Se necesita muchacha* (servant wanted), about the conditions of servants in Peru. It's terrible, because one of them tells how she slept on the floor beside her [female] boss's bed, and when her boss got up in the morning, if her servant hadn't woken up yet, she stepped on her. She just put her feet on her stomach or somewhere else on her body. They tell about their living conditions and the bad treatment they receive. I like to write about women. A few years ago I did a prologue for a book of photographs of the women of Juchitán. I am also working on a book about the carpet makers of Huamantla. There are many single women in that town who dedicate their lives to sanctity, to chastity, and their joy each year is to weave the tunic and dress of the Virgin of Charity. It is a very expensive dress, with pearls, diamonds, and threads of gold. They make carpets with flower petals and they form a path along which they parade this little statue of the Virgin of Charity. All night they walk along this carpet of flowers until everything ends in a drunken binge.
KG: What advice would you give to a young Latin American woman writer who is just starting her career?
EP: A Latin American woman writer is in an extremely privileged situation, because in Europe everything has been said: in France, in Holland, in England everything has been said, everything is written, that's why they write about emotional states, about decisions of the soul. In contrast, Latin America has the enormous privilege of being able to choose; anything that you pick up, there are hundreds of topics swarming underneath. If a young woman goes six blocks from here to a place called the Pedregal de San Francisco and sits all afternoon at that place, she will find 2,200 themes to write about. She will get these topics just by writing about one day there, about the people who go by, the people who go for water, those who close their houses, those who don't close them, the fights, the children who go to school, the condition

of the school, all of that. You can just sit in a grocery store that is very successful here on the Miguel Angel de Quevedo Avenue and listen to the customers, what brands of liquor they buy, how inexpensive they are, and why they ask for them. Bricklayers enter to buy little bottles of tequila and they say that we Mexicans are real drunks. There are so many things, I think that you can find so many themes just by sitting here in Mexico; there are more than enough themes for writing.

KG: That's one reason it has been said that Latin American literature is the most dynamic in the world.

EP: I think that African literature can be the most dynamic in the world, and I think that Japanese literature is also very strange and it can be the most dynamic in the world, and North American literature goes without saying. In Latin America there are countries like Mexico that are tremendously stimulating.

KG: What are your hopes for Mexico in the future?

EP: Well, today in the papers they are talking about the signing of the Free Trade Agreement. I don't know, but you mentioned that there is a lot more traffic, and I feel that there is a great North American invasion of Mexico; every day there are more McDonald's, more Kentucky Fried Chicken, more standardization, our culture is much more uniform. For example, Halloween has replaced the custom of making altars for the dead, which is a beautiful custom. And why has Halloween been more successful? Because on Halloween the older children can ask for handouts. In the United States they have fun asking for candy from door to door; here the children have transformed that into begging. They buy a pumpkin, an orange plastic pumpkin, so that you put handouts in there for them. So a Mexican cultural holiday has been completely transformed into a North American custom.

  I believe that the universities—which are centers of ideas—and the intellectuals have hardly resisted this invasion. This culture is more and more uniform, and there isn't a resistance to the North American culture here. That is a big change. We have completely gone over to the other side. If you see the middle class, if you deal with them a little, [you will see that] their rules and laws belong totally to the consumer society, don't you think so?

INTERVIEW

KG: Yes, and it's a pity because what has been brought here from the United States is not culture, it is fast food, commercialization, whatever brings the most profits to the big corporations.

What would be the ultimate success for you? Do you have a maximum goal or some dream that you would like to realize before you die?

EP: I know that it is very egotistic, but my goal is to make the people around me happy, because to the degree that they are happy, I will be happy. But there also is a radius of action that spreads out and encompasses more people. One time the wife of Alejo Carpentier[3] said something in regard to Cuba that seemed very appropriate. She said that she slept tranquilly in Havana because she felt that everybody had eaten as well as she had. I believe that we all have that same preoccupation in Mexico and in all of the Latin American countries, that people should have greater possibilities, that the personal, loving radius of action should widen to include more and more people.

KG: What would you like written on your tombstone?

EP: On my tombstone! Well, I would like a little chapel like those in small towns, painted yellow and parakeet green, or pink. I wanted to make a chapel like that for Jesusa Palancares, but I haven't been able to because her son always tells me "that's not important." I want to make something small for her and have it say, "Here lies Josefina Bórquez," that's the real name of the woman who gave me her life for the book *Hasta no verte, Jesús mío* (here's to you, Jesus).

KG: Since we have arrived at the grave, I guess this is a good place to stop.

EP: But I haven't told you what I wanted on my tombstone. I have never thought about whether I will say some famous phrase at the hour of death, like, "Light, more light," or a phrase like, "He lived his deceitful life of truths and his true life of deceit."

KG: Thank you, Elena, you can leave us with that paradox.

---

[3] *A contemporary Cuban writer, best known for his novel* The Lost Steps.

Chapter Three

Challenging the Official Story: Elena Poniatowska's *Massacre in Mexico* and *Nada, nadie*

To criticize Caesar
is not to criticize Rome.
To criticize a government
is not to criticize a country.

CARLOS FUENTES,
MASSACRE IN MEXICO

MASSACRE IN MEXICO

THIS COMPLEX TEXT IS A REVEALING CHRONICLE OF THE GOVernment-ordered slaughter of student demonstrators in Mexico City's Plaza de las Tres Culturas (Plaza of Three Cultures) in the district of Tlatelolco on 2 October 1968. Using a discourse/counter-discourse technique in order to undermine the credibility of the official rhetoric, Poniatowska juxtaposes declarations from speeches by President Gustavo Díaz Ordaz and his successor Luis Echeverría[1] with hundreds of eyewitness accounts of the government's actions. She also uses newspaper articles, placards, slogans from buttons, chants, and words captured on a tape recorder. Fragments of songs, poems, and stories from modern Mexico and from different times and places are woven into the intricate tapestry of the text to establish parallels between the present oppression of Mexican citizens and that of other people throughout the history of Latin America. Having provided these heterogeneous means of communication with a historical, social, and political context, she has managed to create a counter-discourse that describes events from the victims' point of view, reveals the author's own powerful voice, and makes a mockery of the pompous, hollow words of the official discourse.

The text is divided into two halves, which simulate the schism produced in so many lives by the massacre. The first half, "Taking to the streets," describes the student movement and the events leading up to 2 October. The second half, "The Night of Tlatelolco," describes the massacre itself and its aftermath. The halves are divided by horrifying photographs of the violence and its consequences.

In the final pages of *Massacre in Mexico*, Poniatowska provides a

---

[1] *Echeverría served in Díaz Ordaz's cabinet as secretary of the interior, in charge of internal security.*

brief chronology of the events described throughout her text.[2] Skirmishes between the police and students began in the summer of 1968 when police intervened in a street fight between students of two different schools. The conflict increased in intensity in late July after a bazooka attack by the riot police on the San Idelfonso Preparatory School, where some demonstrators had taken refuge. Students from various schools organized, forming the CNH *(Comité Nacional de Huelga,* or the *National Strike Committee)* and holding spontaneous rallies on the streets. Students fanned out across Mexico City to hand out flyers that stated their six demands: freedom for all political prisoners, revocation of Article 145 of the Federal Penal Code (the law against "social dissolution," used against David Alfaro Siqueiros and other radicals) (Meyer 664), disbandment of the corps of riot police *(granaderos),* dismissal of the chief and deputy chief of police, indemnities for the families of those killed and injured since the beginning of the conflict, and determination of the responsibility of individual government officials implicated in the bloodshed (53). Underlying this specific agenda was a deep desire for change that connected the Mexicans to the youth protest movements of the sixties in the United States, France, and many other parts of the world.

The students organized massive demonstrations in the streets of Mexico City—their ranks swelled by sympathizers from all walks of life, as well as by curious onlookers—culminating on 27 August with the congregation of 300,000 people in the Central Square, and on 13 September with an equal number of marchers who paraded with gags over their mouths in silent protest. On 18 September the army contravened the national university's autonomy by invading the campus and arresting more than seven hundred people; and on 24 September another confrontation between students and police resulted in many wounded, killed, or arrested.

On 1 October the CNH announced a demonstration the next

---

[2]*While researching these events, I discovered that all the Mexican newspapers from July to December 1968 are not available in the Hemeroteca Nacional, the national newspaper archive in Mexico City. I was told "they do not exist."*

day in the plaza of Tlatelolco, in defiance of a government-ordered "truce" to precede the 1968 Olympic Games in Mexico City, which were to begin on 12 October. This would be the first time that the games were held in Latin America, and in a developing country. The Mexican government had invested between $150 and $200 million (U.S. dollars) on the new metro system, the anthropology museum, the Olympic buildings, tourist facilities, and a clean-up campaign, in order to offer the world an image of a modern, industrialized country. Government officials did not want the games marred by the student protests, and they were particularly fearful of the escalation of the conflict, as increasing numbers of trade union members participated in the demonstrations and foreign correspondents began to arrive in Mexico City before the Olympics. Student groups were divided on the issue of respecting the truce or taking advantage of the international publicity to pressure the government even more.

The 2 October demonstration began peacefully, but was interrupted by a green flare launched from a helicopter, a signal to the soldiers stationed around the square to begin shooting. People panicked and ran from one side of the square to another, trying to escape, but they encountered police blockades and gunfire from all sides. More than four hundred people were killed; thousands were wounded or arrested.

The Mexican newspapers reported the deaths of twenty to thirty people, blaming everybody but the government. The headlines read: "Army Forced to Rout Sharpshooters,"[3] "Shots Exchanged by Sharpshooters and the Army in Tlatelolco," "Criminal Provocation at Tlatelolco Meeting Causes Terrible Bloodshed," "Foreign Interlopers Attempt to Damage Mexico's National Image" (200–201). Due to a massive cover-up, most of the Mexican people outside the capital were unaware of the massacre until they talked to an eyewitness, or read Poniatowska's book.

Massacre in Mexico contradicts the official, whitewashed story, and thus is counter-discursive. It tells the story of the student movement and of the massacre from multiple points of view,

---

[3]"*Sharpshooters*" *is Helen R. Lane's translation of francotiradores, which could also be translated as "snipers."*

using as informants the participants and their families. The text is a complicated ensemble of pretransmitted messages that Poniatowska collected, edited, and organized into different combinations in order to produce a new whole, or an "intertext." This technique, which Poniatowska calls a "collage of voices," creates a textual labyrinth whose bifurcations utilize different types of intertextuality, sometimes supportive and at other times subversive of the original meaning of the excerpts. In general, cases of supportive intertextuality reinforce the ideology expressed in the texts from which the excerpts are taken. Subversive intertextuality, however, changes the message of the original text, adding new connotations or contradicting the intention of the source that is being quoted. As an example of subversive intertextuality, Poniatowska uses irony to undermine the false rhetoric of the ruling party in Mexico, the Institutionalized Revolutionary party, known as the PRI, which has been in power since 1929, having undergone two name changes. The irony is based on a contrast between what is *said* in official speeches by President Gustavo Díaz Ordaz and his successor Luis Echeverría, and what is *done* by government orders, as revealed by eyewitnesses and relatives of the victims. On 1 August 1968, Díaz Ordaz declared in a speech in Guadalajara:

> Peace and calm must be declared in our country. A hand has been extended: it is up to the Mexican citizens to decide whether to grasp this outstretched hand. I have been greatly pained by these deplorable and shameful incidents. Let us not widen the gap between us; let us all refuse to heed the promptings of our false pride, myself included, naturally. (328)

The benevolent and reconciliatory attitude of the government, as indicated by the quotation, is belied by Poniatowska's description of a government-ordered attack on a preparatory school just one day before the speech: "The forces of law and order launch a bazooka attack on the San Idelfonso Preparatory School. Many students from Vocational 2 and Vocational 5 are wounded, and mass arrests are made" (327).

Freedom and education are recurrent themes in the PRI

speeches. A month after his speech in Guadalajara, Díaz Ordaz proclaimed in his Fourth Annual Message (1 September 1968), "Culture is the splendid fruit of freedom" (331). On 30 July 1968 Luis Echeverría, then secretary of internal affairs, declared:

> Mexico is endeavoring to maintain a rule of freedom that is almost without parallel in any other country, by contrast with what happens in dictatorships of whatever political persuasion, or in nations in which chaos and violence rule. (327)

The PRI members also characterized themselves as tolerant and lenient when dealing with the students: "We have been so tolerant that we have been criticized for our excessive leniency," asserted Díaz Ordaz on 1 September 1968 (45).

The Mexican government's words were contradicted by their actions when they sent the army to attack a prep school (327), hired gangs to shoot out the windows and doors of Vocational 7 (80), invaded the National Autonomous University of Mexico (known as UNAM) with tanks and paratrooper transports, and ordered the attack on students during peaceful demonstrations (94). The government's purported leniency with the students is vividly portrayed in the following description that a student gave of his interrogation by the police:

> More punches then, this time right in the balls. The pain was so intense I doubled up and fell to the floor. They stopped punching me then and instead began kicking me from head to foot as I lay there. . . .
> More blows then—in the balls, the belly, the legs. I lay there on the floor screaming with pain and helplessness and rage, with tears streaming down my face. They kept firing questions at me, one after the other. . . .
> More punches, plus electric shocks in my testicles, my rectum, my mouth. And more questions. (107)

In other passages, the students describe the brutal treatment they received both from the police and from federal soldiers, and they tell with lurid details of their torture and deprivation of food, clothes, beds, privacy, light, and all personal effects. The family members of the incarcerated students describe their fright upon visiting the prisoners in jail and seeing them so mistreated, and they tell of their endless and futile efforts to free their relatives.

Torture, incarceration, deprivation, and murder—these were the government's responses to the students' impassioned pleas for a public dialogue. Throughout the hot summer of '68, the students repeatedly sent messages to the government and published statements in national newspapers requesting a dialogue with the president (329). Luis Echeverría proposed, on 22 August 1968, a "frank and peaceful dialogue which will lead to the clarification of the origins and the development of this deplorable problem" (329). Ostensibly accepting the students' request, Echeverría also declared that same day:

> The Government of the Republic is most willing to meet with the representatives of teachers and students at the UNAM, the IPN (the National Polytechnical Institute), and other educational institutions connected with the present problem, in order to exchange views with them and acquaint itself directly with their demands and suggestions, with the aim of definitely resolving the conflict that our capital has experienced in recent weeks. (29)

The president never did meet with the students' and teachers' representatives. Negotiations broke down when the students requested that the dialogue be broadcast on radio and television (Meyer 668). Echeverría claimed, however, that the dialogue had begun when the president addressed the nation:

> It is my opinion that the dialogue has already begun, and that in his Annual Message the President of the Republic discussed in detail each of the six points contained in the petition drawn up by the so-called CNH (the National Strike Committee), as well as other subjects of fundamental interest and transcendent importance. (311)

The photographs in the center of the text *Massacre in Mexico* show soldiers beating students with rifle butts and clubs, lining them up against a wall, and lopping off their hair with bayonets. The photos also depict a group of young people huddled together behind bars, as well as many bloody corpses, including those of pregnant women and young children.

These photographs may be considered visual texts, and as such they contribute to the general process of intertextuality, that is, the combination of many different texts in one unified intertext. They serve here to contradict the political propaganda spouted by the PRI officials, and ironically, they help to create a dialogue in spite of the government's attempt to suppress all opposition and to carry on an unchallenged monologue, as described in the following quote:

> We were fools enough to believe that the government was willing to have a dialogue with us—I say that because when the *granaderos* (riot police) hit us over the head with nightsticks and truncheons they kept saying, "Go ahead and have your dialogue, go ahead and have your dialogue!" So we thought we should be prepared to have a discussion about legal technicalities, but what happened was that they gave us an illegal and antidemocratic clubbing over the head and the dialogue turned out to be a monologue in the form of a 16-year prison sentence and a fine of 1,987,387 pesos. (56)

This quote reveals how the students were silenced, but *Massacre in Mexico* gives them a voice, creating the dialogal space that the Mexican government sought to suppress. Intertextuality may serve to enliven meaning, so that meaning does not become lethargic (Jenny 59), and in this case it constitutes a rejection of the closed book, the open and shut case. The Mexican government wanted to give the appearance of carrying on a dialogue, while actually creating an undisputed monologue. Ironically, the excerpts from the official discourse add energy to the intertext, thus financing their own subversion.

The new meaning created by this subversion actually reinforces the victims' account of events. This account is underscored by the many cases of supportive intertextuality, both explicit and implicit, that criticize governmental repression. Examples of explicit intertextuality include lines from poems by Octavio Paz, Rosario Castellanos, Eduardo Santos, José Carlos Becerra, Juan Bañuelos, and Celia Espinoza de Valle. Poniatowska also quotes from Gabriel García Márquez's *One Hundred Years of Solitude* and Juan Rulfo's *The Plain in Flames*. These excerpts serve to connect the student movement of 1968 to other times and other countries in Latin America that have struggled against oppression. The revolutionary song "La Adelita" appears in the text, transformed into the *"Corrido* to the popular Tita," a tribute to one of the women organizers of the National Strike Committee.[4] Many other of the students' songs and refrains appear, based on radio and television commercials of the time, creating a cultural patchwork quilt whose intricate texture can only be fully appreciated by somebody who lived in Mexico at the time. Poniatowska also includes letters to the editor and the resignation speech made by the rector of the UNAM, who opposed the government's actions. In addition, the author has reproduced pamphlets, slogans from banners and buttons, chants from the demonstrations, tape-recorded voices, and numerous photographs. These heterogeneous means of communication all contribute to the complex process of intertextuality in *Massacre in Mexico*.

There are two possible readings of an intertext: a linear reading in which each segment is accepted as an integral element of the intertext without referring back to the original text, and a nonlinear reading in which a researcher refers back to the original text of each excerpt and analyzes its transformation in the intertext.[5] This second possibility is facilitated in some cases by the immediate identification of the source of the excerpt. Such bifurcations increase the levels of meaning and add historical resonance to the discourse.

An example of nonlinear reading may be offered by the analy-

---

[4]*The corrido is a narrative song, used to communicate news to different parts of Mexico. This form was especially popular during the Mexican Revolution.*
[5]*Laurent Jenny, in "The Strategy of Form" (French Literary Theory Today), refers to these two possible readings as syntagmatic and paradigmatic. A paradigmatic reading suggests an intellectual anamnesis, that is, remembering each of the original texts in its entirety (44).*

CHALLENGING THE OFFICIAL STORY

sis of several Nahuatl poems that are quoted extensively in the middle of Poniatowska's text.[6] The excerpts were chosen for a recital by students in Lecumberri prison, after the massacre of 1968, and they describe a similar massacre that occurred in the same plaza in 1521. The poems, called icnocuicatl (sorrowful songs) and written by the Aztec poets called cuicapicque, were first published in Spanish in Miguel León-Portilla's *Visión de los vencidos*.[7] Excerpts from three different songs are included:

> 1. "The Nahuatl people have been lost" (from *Canciones mexicanas* (Mexican songs, 1523), describes the headlong flight from the Spaniards, the Aztecs' sorrow after defeat, and the capture of their leaders. The poem concludes, "with these deeds / we have lost the Mexican nation."
> 2. "The last days of siege in Tenochtitlan" (from the Anonymous Manuscript of Tlatelolco, 1528) depicts the miserable condition of the indigenous people under siege by the Spaniards, and the prices put on the heads of the Aztec leaders.
> 3. "The ruin of the Tenochca and Tlatelolca people" (also from *Canciones mexicanas*) was part of a collection of melodramatic poems that were intended for theatrical presentation. They tell the entire history of the Conquest, but in *Visión de los vencidos,* León-Portilla only included some of the most emotional poems about the destruction of the Nahuatl people.

As quoted in *Massacre in Mexico,* the poems begin in medias res, with a provocative description of putrefaction and spilled blood:

> *Worms are crawling through the streets*
> *and the squares and the walls*
> *are spattered with brains. . . .*
> *The water is red,*

---

[6] *Nahuatl is the language spoken by the Aztecs and still used by some indigenous people in central Mexico today.*
[7] *León-Portilla edited and published the original Nahuatl texts. The Spanish translation is by Angel María Garibay. The text has also been translated into English, with the title Broken Spears: The Aztec Account of the Conquest of Mexico (Boston: Beacon, 1962).*

ELENA PONIATOWSKA

> as though it were dyed,
> and when we drink it it is as though
> we were drinking water
> with rock salt in it. (166)

There are three more verses from the same poem, and then alternating excerpts from all three poems. Using the numbers in the above list to identify the poems, the order of their appearance in the intertext is: 2, 3, 1, 2, 3. This rotation does not have a chaotic effect; on the contrary, it produces a certain thematic unity and a relatively chronological progression. The poems first describe the horrible conditions and the destruction of war, then the death or capture of the Aztec leaders and the general surrender to the Spaniards, and finally the end of war. The last two lines repeat the ominous chorus: the war against the Mexican people continues.

Structurally, *Visión de los vencidos* and *Massacre in Mexico* are similar in that they both combine many different accounts of the same event, with alternating voices that narrate and reiterate the story from various points of view, all unified by a central theme and organized in a loosely chronological order. Both texts alternate detailed descriptions with brief summaries of the action that serve to orient the reader and keep the story in focus.

Poniatowska establishes a parallel between the two massacres based on the similarity of the two events, the geographic location, and several elements that are emphasized in the accounts of both massacres: the point of view of the victims, the use of foreshadowing, exchanges of messages, intimidation of the students/Aztecs with threats and guns, inferior weapons of the victims, the use of ambush, the flowing of blood, tears and rain, the torture of prisoners, and the presence of a god figure in control whose divine justice has become divine revenge. For the Aztecs, this figure was Tlatoani, the Giver of Life, whom they thought had betrayed them. For the students, the figure is President Díaz Ordaz, who is ironically called the Giver of Life (23).

In León-Portilla's text, most of the authors are anonymous; in Poniatowska's work, the narrators are identified, but there are so many of them, and their individual stories are so fragmented and scattered throughout the text, that the impression created is of an anonymous, collective voice. In both books it is the voice of the common people that speaks from the victims' point of view, presenting the other side of a story already told by the Spaniards in one case, and by the Mexican newspapers and official releases of the PRI in the other case.

By choosing to recite the Aztec poems in prison, the Mexican students reveal a historical awareness that was not widespread in the student movements of the sixties. Student protesters in the United States were principally iconoclastic and antihistorical: anybody over the age of thirty was suspect, and there was a conscious effort to create a rupture in historical continuity. The Mexican students, in contrast, drew on Marxist theory to protest a corrupt regime and tried to reconnect with their indigenous past, which added historical meaning to their protest. This same historical awareness is present among the volunteer rescue workers who narrate their stories in Poniatowska's *Nada, nadie,* the story of the earthquake that destroyed large areas of Mexico City in 1985. Many of the same people were involved in both the student movement of 1968 and the rescue work of 1985.

Poniatowska chose the Aztec poems and direct quotes from other literary works and interwove them with the personal testimonies to enhance the aesthetic, ideological, and historical value of her text, just as an artist painstakingly arranges bits and pieces of pictures in order to create a montage. In this sense she has created a literary work, although Octavio Paz calls it "an extraordinary piece of reporting" (in the Introduction to *Massacre in Mexico,* p. vii), and it has been compared to the new journalism popularized by Truman Capote's *In Cold Blood* (Pedén 45). Although Poniatowska's own voice is subordinated to that of her informants, she does set the tone for the book in the preface:

> They come down [the streets of Mexico City], laughing, students walking arm in arm in the demonstration, in as festive a mood as if they were going to a street fair; carefree boys and girls who do not know that tomorrow, and the day after, their dead bodies will be lying swollen in the rain, after a fair where the guns in the shooting gallery are aimed at them. (3)

ELENA PONIATOWSKA

This contrast between the gaiety before and the dead bodies after the slaughter highlights the horror of the event. The comparison of the students with mechanical ducks in a shooting gallery is a powerful metaphor, full of recrimination. Poniatowska also expresses her own opinion by choosing which material to include, and by quoting an article that she wrote about the attack on political prisoners by common prisoners (151–53). Her own personal tragedy—the loss of a brother in a car accident in December 1968—is barely mentioned beyond the book's dedication, but she mourns this loss by recording the sorrow of hundreds of people. At the beginning of the second half of the book, she expresses her gratitude to those who shared their innermost feelings with her. Poniatowska's presence is also felt when several of the speakers address her as Elena, and she reveals her own piquant sense of humor when she quotes a postal clerk who asserts: "It's the mini-skirt that's to blame" (82).

Humor is hard to find, however, in this somber testimonial. It is not until ten years later, in a chapter on the student movement included in her book *Fuerte es el silencio* (strong is the silence), that Poniatowska can speak of some positive consequences of the violent repression. The student movement was the detonator that broke the traditional Mexican mutism and allowed the resentment handed down from generation to generation to be expressed. According to Poniatowska, this explosion destroyed the official image of Mexico as a country above the rest of Latin America and thus incapable of the brutal repression that has plagued this continent for centuries. One measure of the people's discontent was the unusually low percentage of the population who voted in the 1970 elections (64 percent of registered voters), which was considered a slap in the face to the official PRI candidate, Luis Echeverría.

The massacre provoked the formation of new leftist organizations in Mexico and served as a catalyst for the radicalization of important intellectuals such as Carlos Fuentes, Carlos Monsiváis, and José Emilio Pacheco. The student movement provided leadership and consciousness-raising opportunities for women such as Ana Ignacia Rodríguez (La Nacha) and Roberta Avendaño (La Tita), who were both immortalized in *Massacre in Mexico*. So much pressure was put on President Echeverría that he felt compelled to include young people in both state and federal government in unprecedented numbers.

Like the lives of many individuals, Mexican history was divided by the massacre: before and after 2 October 1968. Alfredo Cuéllar, the president of the student organization of the National School of Physical Education in 1968, an eyewitness of the massacre and presently an administrator at California State University in Fresno, said to me in an interview in 1990: "I think that [the massacre] is the most important political event of my life. I think that Tlatelolco is present in everything that I write and say now, directly or indirectly." The lessons learned, however bitter, have not been forgotten. The dialogue established by Poniatowska's counter-discourse continues, as new articles appear and new movies are made about the student movement and the massacre of 1968.[8] Many recent books have references to Tlatelolco, which indicates that the tragedy still lives in the collective consciousness of the Mexican people.[9] One such book is Poniatowska's *Nada, nadie.*

NADA, NADIE: LAS VOCES DEL TEMBLOR

Seventeen years after the Tlatelolco massacre, another major tragedy occurred. On 19 September 1985, at 7:19 A.M., an earthquake caught Mexico City by surprise. The quake measured 8.0 on the Richter scale (which has nine degrees of intensity) and lasted two full minutes. It was followed by an aftershock a day later that measured 5.6. Various sources reported drastically different tolls: from 2,000 to 7,160 wounded; from 100,000 to 250,000 left homeless; and anywhere from 2,000 to 500,000 missing or dead. Most people believe, however, that there were about 10,000 people killed. Poniatowska's *Nada, nadie* is the

---

[8]See, for example, the three articles on the massacre published in the 3 October 1988 issue of *Proceso* (Mexico City), or the 1989 movie *Rojo amanecer* (Red Dawn), produced by Cinematográfica Sol.
[9]See Young, Dolly J., "Mexican Literary Reactions to Tlatelolco 1968," *Latin American Research Review* 20.2 (1985): 71–85.

personal account behind those numbers. It is a story of anguish, anger, and helplessness, as well as uncommon heroism and generosity. It is narrated by countless survivors of the disaster, those left without homes, without family members, without identification and thus with no official existence. They tell of the Boy Scout who brought a baby out of a collapsed building, only to die when a wall fell on him after he returned to the rubble for another child. They reveal the heartbreak of a mother whose five-year-old daughter was raped by a soldier who was sent to "protect" the area. This book also touches upon the ridiculous and the sublime: a seventy-year-old woman refused to be rescued until a volunteer brought her a dress and lipstick; articles donated by the Mexican elite included thirty wigs, Halloween costumes, swimsuits, and even a bride's dress; and one person, surprised by the help sent from all over the world, declared that Mexico didn't know it was so well loved.

With these diverse elements, Poniatowska has created a book of stark contrasts, a text that details destruction and death but offers hope and strength. The lessons learned are highlighted again by the author's discourse/counter-discourse technique. Very little space is dedicated to the official discourse of the PRI, because the politicians had ample coverage by the media, but Poniatowska does repeat enough of their speeches and announcements so that a reader unfamiliar with the events of 1985 could understand their position. Much of the text consists of a detailed counter-discourse, which tells the story from the point of view of the *damnificados* (the condemned, those left homeless), and is mainly a negative reaction to the official story. The author also has created a powerful alternative discourse, both personal and collective, which is much more positive and life-affirming. This alternative discourse depicts the bravery and solidarity of the people and offers hope for the future. Although the seeds of this alternative discourse were present in *Massacre in Mexico,* it is much more developed in *Nada, nadie.* In contrast, intertextuality, which plays such an important role in the former book, is not prominent in the latter work, in which she reproduces other people's testimony but does not quote well-known authors' poems, short stories, and novels. In other words, with only one exception (which will be discussed later in this chapter), the reader of *Nada, nadie* could not go back to the original sources of the excerpts in order to analyze how they have been transformed in the intertext.

Poniatowska establishes the discourse/counter-discourse technique in the first few pages of *Nada, nadie*, although she begins with counter-discourse: an eyewitness account of the devastating effects of the earthquake, with references to the severe problems that plagued Mexico City before the disaster. Various narrators criticize the government for not controlling the population explosion, the unorganized urban sprawl, the transportation problems, and the world's worst air pollution. These problems, as well as the substandard construction of government buildings, many of which collapsed, exacerbated the consequences of the quake. Ironically, it took an earthquake to expose violations in the building codes, as well as more serious human rights violations as evidenced by the torture chamber that was discovered in the basement of the secret police building. To a much greater degree than in *Massacre in Mexico*, the official discourse is presupposed: it exists in a pretextual space and it is assumed that the reader has access to this space. Government officials are only quoted a few times, and usually to point out something particularly outrageous, such as when President Miguel de la Madrid refused aid from the rest of the world:

> We are prepared to deal with this situation and we do not need external help. Mexico has enough resources, and with the people and government united, we will make progress. We are thankful for your good intentions, but we are self-sufficient. (24)[10]

---

[10] All quotes are from Nada, nadie: Las voces del temblor (Mexico: Ediciones Era, 1988), and have been translated by me. Due to the length of this book, the original Spanish is included in parentheses only when a word lacks a clear translation. The reader may refer to the original text, using the page numbers given in parentheses.

The counter-discourse throughout the text reveals the government's lack of foresight and preparation for a disaster. This information is included in personal testimonies and is not organized in an obvious contrapuntal order. Poniatowska has arranged the text in a vaguely chronological manner, beginning with the earthquake itself, describing its consequences, and ending with some reflections on lessons learned. However, there are many repetitions and flashbacks, as different people tell their stories, and the reader must play an active role, piecing together the puzzle and reconstructing the various points made by the government with the corresponding counterpoints made by the people.

The government's plan had the mysterious name DN-III, and in practical terms it consisted of sending troops to cordon off the disaster areas, ostensibly to facilitate rescue missions and to protect the buildings from looters. In *Nada, nadie,* numerous witnesses testify to the fact that the soldiers actually impeded the rescue in many cases and were the worst looters in other cases. The plan DN-III, according to several of the narrators, was a repressive plan, a plan to control the people, not to save them. The police force had dogs trained to control riots, but no dogs to search out survivors. The government did not provide maps of the disaster areas, and there were no floor plans of the destroyed buildings to facilitate rescue missions. Volunteers did not know where they were needed, and once they arrived at a crumbled building, there was nobody in charge to organize their efforts. The soldiers were provided with rifles, not rescue equipment. Volunteers had to produce their own picks and shovels, and much of the rubble was removed in buckets. Some of the volunteers were arrested or beaten up, just for trying to help. This chaos prevailed for days after the catastrophe, and many victims died who could have been saved if there had been an organized emergency plan that used the help of local volunteers and foreign experts, who were finally allowed to enter the country.

Two weeks after the earthquake, Poniatowska attended a meeting of the National Reconstruction Commission, where she recorded some of the official rhetoric: "Mexico never shows its virtue more than when it faces adversity," "We know how

CHALLENGING THE OFFICIAL STORY

to unite in a common effort," "The leadership of the President [is] serene and firm" (99). At this meeting, President De la Madrid called for a restructuring of national life and declared his interest in creating a dialogue with the heroic young people of Mexico. No mention was made of devising better emergency plans, no testimony was given by the impoverished people most affected by the disaster, and the corruption that contributed to the disaster and crippled the relief efforts was not denounced.

In contrast, corruption was a major theme in the testimony of many of the survivors. Violations to the building codes were routinely ignored by the government, resulting in the collapse of many buildings that should have been condemned, including the Nuevo León in the plaza of Tlatelolco. Volunteers who arrived at the Mexico City airport watched in amazement as customs officials confiscated their rescue equipment and even their personal luggage, including return-trip airplane tickets. Much of the food and clothing sent for the homeless never reached them. Some government workers discovered minor ways to increase their income: at times people had to pay tolls to enter the disaster areas, others had to pay bribes in order to recover the cadavers of their relatives, and at rescue sites water was sold at one thousand pesos a liter. Survivors trying to recover valuables or bury their dead discovered a bureaucratic nightmare. Government workers sent them from one building to another, made them wait hours on end, and told them repeatedly to come back tomorrow. One victim described this experience as a "viacrucis," referring to the torment of the stations of the cross.

Disregard for human suffering, and even for the right to life, was displayed with impunity. In the interest of clearing the streets, some buildings were bulldozed away in spite of the possibility that survivors were still trapped in the rubble. One witness reported:

> On the corner of Versalles and Chapultepec Avenue, on 19 September, an army lieutenant was trying to get people off the rubble with gross insults and violence. He had received orders to clear [the people] off and to demolish

the construction in spite of the presence of some possible survivors. The relatives' pleading was of no use.

Where were those soldiers raised? The army demolished the building and a living person whose cries everybody heard, died, a victim of arbitrariness and power. (183)

Another witness reported arriving at Datamex and finding seventy-two people who had recently died because they were trapped in a building that was demolished with heavy machinery. "Those people could have been saved if there were more respect for human life," he commented (241).

Poniatowska strengthens her counter-discourse by establishing a parallel between the earthquake and the 1968 massacre in Tlatelolco. Some of the references are implied, perhaps even unintentionally, such as with the president's suggestion of a dialogue with the heroic young people of Mexico (like the dialogue requested by the students in 1968). Other references are obvious. One of the buildings that collapsed due to substandard construction was the Nuevo León, in Tlatelolco. The residents had complained that the building was falling apart. Some had even propped up their walls with wooden beams. The government sent some experts to investigate, and they declared the building to be "the safest building not only in Tlatelolco but in all of Mexico City" (253). The building was totally destroyed in the earthquake, as shown on the fourth page of photos in *Nada, nadie,* with the caption: "First there was the massacre in Tlatelolco, now it is the Nuevo León building: corruption is also a crime."

The parallel is established with the first description of the plaza of Tlatelolco after the earthquake: "Like seventeen years ago, the Plaza of Three Cultures is a battleground, in which they have improvised tents where incomplete families share their misfortune with their neighbors" (20). Later in the text, Poniatowska emphasizes an element she had mentioned in *Massacre in Mexico,* the shoes scattered around on the ground: "Like on October 2 [1968], when the Plaza of the Three Cultures in Tlatelolco was covered with shoes, like trampled flowers!" (289). Many of the people who volunteered to help in 1985 had participated in the student movement of 1968, and one man declared: "I have two big impacts engraved in my mind, this one of September 19 [1985], and the [tragedy of] '68"(232).

When Poniatowska describes her anticipation of the meeting of the National Reconstruction Commission, she expresses what she hopes will happen, using the future tense in an interior monologue. One of her expectations is that they will honor the dead, recalling the words of the Anonymous Manuscript of Tlatelolco, a text she quotes in *Massacre in Mexico* to establish the parallel between the Spaniards' massacre of the Aztecs in 1521 and the government's ambush of the students in 1968 in the same plaza. In an exceptional case of intertextuality, she quotes a description of the destruction in 1521:

> In the roads lie broken spears; hair is spread everywhere. Roofless are the houses, red with blood are the walls. Worms are crawling through the streets and the squares, and the walls are spattered with brains. The water is red, as though it were dyed, and when we drink it, it is as though we were drinking water with rock salt in it. In our anxiety we struck the adobe walls and we were left with a network of holes. (95)

By using this quote, the center of which is also quoted in *Massacre in Mexico,* Poniatowska reinforces her counter-discourse by drawing parallels between the disasters of 1521, 1968, and 1985. The implication is that in all three instances the people were victims of those in power. The unifying elements are greed, violence, and the desire for control.

Poniatowska had other expectations for the Reconstruction Commission meeting, also: they would hug each other, they would listen to the stories of the *damnificados,* the volunteers would report on their progress, they would hear how things would be different in the future, and they would each leave the meeting with a task to complete. By the end of the meeting she was totally disillusioned: the politician's empty rhetoric had nothing to do with what was happening on the street; the protagonists of the tragedy were not allowed to speak. Poniatowska enlivens her counter-discourse by contrasting the reality on the street with the "official" place within the meeting, compounding the spacial contrast with a temporal one:

> Outside, "operation ant" [digging with picks and shovels] does not cease, each minute that passes is precious; covered with dust, the rescuers stop to drink water; here under the umbrella [the roof of the museum], time is the same as before the earthquake, political time: slow, rhetorical, anachronistic, devious, personalist and usurious. . . . [the speakers weave together] phrases that don't mean anything . . . and nobody says what we hope to hear. (96–97)

In both *Massacre in Mexico* and *Nada, nadie,* contrast and irony are two of the strongest weapons in Poniatowska's counter-discourse. In the latter text, one of her informants reveals that in preparation for a visit by President De la Madrid to a disaster area, all rescue work was halted and the machines were turned off because they had to sweep the street. Four days after the earthquake, a newspaper announced the grand bazaar of Carmen Romano, wife of the former president José López Portillo. She was selling her treasures that didn't fit in her house, including several microwave ovens, twelve pianos, and some oriental rugs. No mention is made as to who would profit from the sale. Poniatowska's description of the newspaper that day highlights the contrast:

> Between the photos of buildings tumbled in the streets like great prehistoric animals, the ruins that are now our urban landscape, the zones of tragedy, the plaza of the Three Cultures, the Multifamily-building Juárez, the Medical Center, was the announcement of the "garage sale" of jewels, furniture and porcelain from various centuries, by doña Carmen, wife of the ex-president of the Republic. (228)

Irony is also evident when Poniatowska expresses her surprise to find a government engineer who is doing his job well. Everybody expresses respect for him, and the author comments, "I can't get over my astonishment" (*"No salgo de mi asombro"*) (231). Poniatowska allows the engineer to tell his side of the story, permitting some of the official discourse to enter her text. The engineer defends the government's decision to keep "curious people" away from the rescue sites, and declares that his men are honest and that they are not stealing anything. The inclusion of this testimony makes Poniatowska's text more believable, because she does not insist that all the government workers are corrupt. She treats this engineer with respect, although she expresses the opinion that he does not know what all the other workers are doing. By providing some balance and by expressing surprise upon encountering an obvious exception, this dialogue ultimately reinforces the counter-discourse in *Nada, nadie*.

Another powerful weapon in Poniatowska's arsenal is the use of single phrases at the end of sections. After long descriptive or narrative paragraphs, the author often closes with a single sentence that hits the reader like a whip. These sentences are direct or indirect negations of the official discourse, as they express desperation and rage with very few words. Because of the Spanish language's tolerance of, and even insistence upon, double negatives, as many as four negative words—or even more—may appear in a short sentence. For the sake of illustration, all the negative words have been translated as negatives in the following examples:

> —I am no longer nobody. (*Yo ya no soy nadie.*) (18)
> —I am left without nobody, and without nothing, young man. (*Me quedé sin nadie y sin nada, señito.*) (80)
> —No, nothing is not happening. (*No, si no pasa nada.*) (64)
> —Hey, didn't nobody come? (*Oye, ¿no vino nadie?*) (95)
> —In Mexico nobody takes responsibility for nothing. (*En México nadie se responsabiliza de nada.*) (83)

This technique, besides contributing to the counter-discourse, illustrates the title of the book.

A more gentle technique used by Poniatowska is humor. This is a transitional technique, leading out of counter-discourse and into the more positive, alternative discourse. The author finishes her section on the "reconstruction" meeting with a joke based on the double meaning of the word *incapacidad* (disability, or incompetence): "—Why did the President go to Social Security [the health insurance building]? —To get three more years of *incapacidad*" (101). To begin her section based on newspapers published outside Mexico City, the author quotes *El siglo* (the century): "Just as hurricanes are named, so should earthquakes be named; the one on the nineteenth could be called 'Luis Echeverría' and the one on the twentieth could be called 'López Portillo' (both former presidents of Mexico)" (101).

Humor is also evident in a rescuer's story of the old woman who refused to leave her crumbled home:

> I also had to deal with a woman who didn't want to come out. I found her sitting [in the ruins] and when I told her that we were going to get her out she said:
> —I am not an old tramp (*coscolina*). How am I going to leave like this?
> She was naked. She didn't have on outer clothing. I told her that I would get her a dress. When I came back she said to me:
> —My lipstick.
> —What did you lose, ma'am?
> —My lipstick. I have to paint my lips.
> She was an old woman, about 70. And such a flirt.
> I went to get a tube of lipstick for her, I don't know where, and I took it to her. Only then did she agree to come out. (257)

This is alternative discourse, the people looking at themselves with humor and warmth, with caring. Not as numbers that can be added or subtracted with ease, not as an amorphous group of *damnificados*. One of the major strengths of Poniatowska's style is her ability to rescue individuals from the collective mass, to tell a personal story that reflects everybody else's tragedy, but a story with a name and an identity. The fortitude of Dr. Marta Torres, for example, energizes the alternative discourse. Trapped for six days in the General Hospital, with a forty-ton concrete beam crushing her leg, the doctor aided in her own rescue by shouting detailed information about where she was and what was on top of her. Lying in a narrow tunnel and engulfed by the smell of decomposing flesh, a team of doctors, with Marta's encouragement, amputated her leg before dragging her to safety.

Another story of strength is that of the seamstresses, whose boss ordered the rescue workers to extricate the machinery first, then try to save the women. Poniatowska comments:

> The fortitude, or should I say, the grandeur of our women is more and more impressive. Rosario, Chonita, doña Lupe, Cata,

CHALLENGING THE OFFICIAL STORY

Romelia Navarro, Elena Rosales who with no more armor
than her red sweater is confronting the boss, Elías Serur. (64)

Before the earthquake, these women were packed into substandard buildings with insufficient light and ventilation. They worked very long hours, with no benefits and no time off, even for illness. Galvanized by mistreatment and neglect after the earthquake, the seamstresses formed a union that is still in operation, a very positive result of the disaster that has significantly changed these women's lives. Six hundred seamstresses died. The remaining seamstresses now work under better conditions, with better pay and more respect.

Another very positive aspect of the quake's aftermath was the cooperation and solidarity of the people, in spite of the government's attempts to keep them from organizing. Faced with the leadership void after the quake, the people took to the streets themselves and formed grassroots organizations that not only helped rescue people from buildings but also provided food and water for rescuers and victims of the disaster. Volunteers came from all walks of life, some of them traveling from distant states and even from different countries. Octavio Paz is quoted as saying, "Mexicans felt that they were not alone, that they were not behind or in a corner of history, but that they formed a part of the world" (173).

Donated clothing, medicine, and blankets overwhelmed the receiving centers.[11] People contributed what they could: a little money, their one change of clothes, their time and energy. Actors and singers performed for the victims in the makeshift shelters. Members of youth gangs pitched in and surprised everybody with their willingness to help. The strength and spirit of the young people were a source of hope. One informant declared:

> Perhaps I am wrong, but I perceived our young people to be taller, stronger, braver than those of previous generations, more

---

[11] *The people of Mexico City reciprocated in October of 1987, when there was an earthquake near Santa Cruz. So many donations were sent from the Mexican capital that most of them had to be shipped elsewhere for storage, or to benefit the victims of other disasters.*

organized. This mobilization didn't occur when the Angel of Independence fell 28 years ago. The young people of all the neighborhoods, from Santa Julia, Guerrero, San Angel, even Polanco and las Lomas, are making a united effort. (130)

An important element of the alternative discourse is the incorporation of lessons learned into the collective consciousness. Many informants talked about the need to be more prepared, to have evacuation drills, to insist on adherence to building codes, to protect themselves in the future. One man asked, "Will we learn the lesson well, or are we going to continue haphazardly, just to see what happens to us, telling ourselves 'that's life' ('*ni modo manito*'), it was our turn?" (186) One indication that this consciousness persisted was the strong showing of the government's opposition in the 1988 national elections. Leftist parties' share of the votes increased from 9.4 percent in 1982 to 23.4 percent in 1988 (Barry 33).

The alternative discourse in *Nada, nadie* also describes positive effects of the experience on the volunteer workers. Many experienced a profound change:

> I saw the eyes of those who had been with us and they were different, very distinct from the eyes of all the other people. A young woman told me afterwards that it was because they were looking inside, I don't know what it was, but it was a new posture of ours when faced with something different, I don't know whether to call it mystical, philosophical or marxist-scientific; I believe, the truth is I don't know what it could be, but it was like a very cathartic state, a constant catharsis. (142)

Other workers reported a newfound respect, a tremendous love of life, the desire to live and to help others live. Mexicans discovered how much they love Mexico, and that they never want to leave. They vowed to make the volunteer brigades permanent, to systematize their efforts, to continue with the newfound cooperation, to keep the energy flowing. Poniatowska concludes:

> Nevertheless one can find something positive in all this. We ought to question the old feeling of inferiority that we Mexicans have. We Mexicans are not inadequate, the

system is. We saw that if we work together we can do it well. (172)

A poem that was printed and handed out on street corners offers consolation to the dead and hope to the living:

> *Your death, comrade, has not been in vain.*
> *Because it is the fertilizer that nourishes our hope.*
> *It is the banner of our struggle.*
> *Difficult and hard days await us, but we will know how to respond,*
> *We assure you.* (182)

When faced with difficult days and with the greatest tragedy of all, the death of a family member, how do you put your life back together? That is the subject of one of the sections in *Nada, nadie*, and it constitutes an important element in the alternative discourse. It goes beyond words of hope and solidarity to get to something deeper and at the same time more practical: how life goes on after the disaster. To answer this question, Poniatowska refers to her mother, who lost a son in December of 1968. How did she manage to get up each day? How could she start, put one foot in front of the other? The author remembers that once her mother told her that landscapes had helped her a lot, to see great barren plains along the edge of a highway, the sky stretching out above, and "the pinetrees that go up the mountainslopes, forming green pyramids that point upwards" (252). Poniatowska's mother also told her that she felt that her son was still with her, she felt him by her side, and within herself. This was something that many of the survivors needed to feel.

And Poniatowska helped them feel that, as she helps the reader. She identifies intimately with those who suffer. Speaking with a grieving mother, Gloria Guerrero, she affirms that she will never forget the woman's face, she will die with her painful eyes engraved on her forehead, like those of Judith, of Salomón Reyes, of Andrés Escoto, and of so many others. "Because if the other exists, I exist," she explains, "and if he died I also die even though I may be walking around and putting one foot in front of the other" (248). Poniatowska's identification with the grieving mother is so intense that she sees herself in the woman's face:

ELENA PONIATOWSKA

> And [I also die] even though I might pass a comb through my hair or even take out lipstick to form another mouth on mine, a mouth which now moves in front of me, the eyes that now cloud over in front of my eyes, the thin skin which reddens, the grimace of crying, the nervous hands that try to stem the crying and those trembling, salty lips that rain salt and are distorted and they are mine and they are Gloria Guerrero's. Gloria Guerrero, Gloria Guerrero, whose 5-and-a-half-year-old daughter Alondra died. (249)

Thus Elena Poniatowska's voice is heard both in the counter-discourse, as she contradicts the politician's rhetoric and allows many others to do the same, and in the alternative discourse, as she adds her voice to the many expressions of hope and affirmation. Her voice is more than just one in the crowd, however. Her voice guides the narrative, gives it depth and shape, and by means of her own powerful identification with the suffering survivors, she pulls the reader into the same identification. And even though the text is so fragmented that there is no real character development, there is a protagonist whose identity is felt throughout all the stories, someone whose presence underlies the anecdotes: the person who records the stories, the narrator who pulls all the narratives together. And that protagonist, of course, is Elena Poniatowska. This text is not fiction, but it has narrative qualities, and those characteristics bring the story to life and make it more powerful.

The counter-discourse in both *Massacre in Mexico* and *Nada, nadie* uses contrast, irony, humor, eye-witness accounts, and intertextuality to contradict the government's rhetoric. In her later work, Poniatowska assails the official discourse by using short, single sentences with multiple negatives, strategically placed at the ends of sections.

Nada, nadie, published seventeen years after *Massacre in Mexico,* is a more mature work. Poniatowska's voice is more evident and more self-assured, her narrative techniques are more developed, and she is more open about her feelings and opinions. Therefore, the reader is more drawn into *Nada, nadie.* The latter text also offers a well-developed alternative discourse—only the seeds of which are present in the text on Tlatelolco—that incorporates humor, empathy, and collective wisdom into a more positive expression of the Mexican people. Written ten years after the massacre, *Fuerte es el silencio* is a transitional work that both offers a postscript to *Massacre in Mexico* and prefigures *Nada, nadie* by analyzing some of the positive outcomes of the student movement, and by offering more of her own commentary. All three of these texts help to establish a dialogue with a government that has been intent on monologue.

Poniatowska's message of hope and solidarity includes identification with those who suffer, emphasis on lessons learned, perspective gained through experience, and a profound, unshakeable love of Mexico and life itself. One of the narrators of *Nada, nadie* explains: "I didn't want to have eyes to see what I saw, but if the things that my eyes saw really happened in my native city, I would not change places with anybody and I am glad to be here, with everybody" (309). That is Poniatowska's ultimate message; it is a tribute to a country and a people she loves. This message needs to be intuited; it needs to be felt, not simply read. It is a message that passes almost imperceptibly from author to reader, making the reader one with the author, and one with the victims. It is the emotional content of Poniatowska's alternative discourse.

PART II
ANGELES MASTRETTA

Chapter Four
Introduction

I write searching for pleasure
and for the present
and for the time for loving
for laughter
and for reason to be laughing.

I write from the doubt
irrevocably pinned to my waist
from solitude and companionship

I write to be alive.

Angeles Mastretta,
Out of the Volcano

I WAITED A LONG TIME IN THE SPACIOUS, GLASSED-IN LIVING ROOM in Mexico City, gazing at the photograph of Angeles Mastretta with her two children at the beach. In the photo the wind was blowing her hair over her face, and she looked so happy—so alive—as she embraced her son and her daughter. There was also an elegant portrait of her that emphasized her enormous eyes and her thick brown hair. A large-leafed plant was in the fireplace, and the chimney served as a frame for a huge painting of Cholula's pyramid, the top of which was graced by a Catholic church: a fitting metaphor for Mexico's layers of history and culture. Many other works of art graced the walls and surfaces, including a statue of a dancing woman, whose frozen movement seemed to capture the raw tension underneath Angeles's writing. A glass table was adorned with luxurious books and magazines, continuous feasts for the eyes and the intellect. A television soap opera was playing in another room, and delicious smells were emanating from the kitchen. Into this setting strode the woman who reigns over this household: Angeles Mastretta. She has been best described by the author and translator Margaret Sayers Pedén:[1]

> She is a whirlwind of charm. It is easy to picture this intelligent and attractive woman as the host of a television talk show or as a famous Italian screen star. There is much about her that still suggests her Italian heritage (her paternal grandfather arrived in Mexico in 1910): the cheekbones, the rich chestnut hair, the animated gestures, the husky, sensual voice. She is at the same time avowedly Mexican. (87)

---

[1] *Margaret Sayers Pedén is a professor of Spanish at the University of Missouri–Columbia. She has contributed chapters to* Voices of Protest, *and she has translated many works from Spanish to English, including Carlos Fuentes's* Terra Nostra *and* Hydra Head.

ANGELES MASTRETTA

That was the woman I met the first time I was invited to her home, in 1991. The following year, I was privileged to see a different side of Angeles, a more personal and intimate side. This time she was more subdued, suffering from an ulcer and from exhaustion and wearing no makeup. Because she had already thoroughly impressed me the previous summer, she no longer felt compelled to project that polished image, and I was very pleased to meet Angeles the person, rather than Angeles the star. She looked tired, but still quite attractive, and much more real. Nevertheless, she brought her cosmetics with her and proceeded to put them on in my presence, beginning by curling her eyelashes with the edge of a spoon. As I witnessed her transformation, she explained to me that she was painting herself so as not to insult/attack me (*"para no agredirte"*), because ugliness is an aggression against the beholder. I recognized in this statement an explanation of her fictional strategies, as well as the creation of her public image. Hard edges were softened and reality was safely covered up with a playful yet dramatic mask.

This is a survival strategy in the high-powered publishing and political world in which Angeles operates. She has had incredible success with her novel *Arráncame la vida* (translated as *Mexican Bolero*), which tells the story of the wife of a powerful politician in the state of Puebla in the 1930s and 1940s. This novel has been translated into twelve languages and has run at least twenty editions in Spanish, with more than 250,000 copies sold.

Angeles is married to Héctor Aguilar Camín, the director of the prestigious cultural magazine *Nexos* (connections) and author of many historical and fictional books.[2] Known in some circles as the cultural czar of Mexico, Aguilar Camín has been successfully integrated into the Mexican political elite. Her husband's increasing visibility may be one reason that Angeles

---

[2]*Héctor Aguilar Camín (1946–), whose recent works* Morir en el golfo *(to die in the gulf [1985]) and* A la sombra de la Revolución *(in the shadow of the Revolution [1989]) can be found on the front table of most Mexican bookstores, has been called "perhaps the most outstanding of the pro-Salinas intellectuals" (Guillermoprieto 101). He is the supervisor and coauthor of a new official history textbook for Mexico's elementary schools, which vindicates the policies of the dictator Porfirio Díaz.*

INTRODUCTION

has embedded her criticism of the Mexican political and familial systems within a delightfully entertaining novel, in which all of the names of historical figures are changed. In spite of this subterfuge, Angeles has had to withstand much criticism of her portrayal of governmental officials and the social elite of Puebla, and the reviews in Mexico of her work have been mixed. The journalist Braulio Peralta has praised her characters for their authenticity, and the feminist critic Aralia López González has pointed out her protagonist's solidarity with women of different social classes.[3] Martha Robles, however, in her two-volume study of Mexican women writers, claims that Angeles makes no contribution to Mexican letters, and of *Mexican Bolero* she writes: "Here everything is linear: the life, the story, and the course of events. There is no surprise or poetry, no original character or situation" (323).[4] Ironically, the reviews published in the United States have been overwhelmingly positive, perhaps because nobody feels particularly implicated by Angeles's criticism. Praise of *Mexican Bolero* has been published in the *Los Angeles Times,* the *Philadelphia Inquirer, Kirkus Reviews,* and the prestigious journal *Hispania*.[5] In the *Los Angeles Times* review, Carolyn See asserts that for "a woman with brains, or anyone at all interested in Latin America, this book is a find, a golden nugget, a kaleidoscope, a day at the beach" (E8).

Angeles was born in October of 1949 in the city and state of Puebla, Mexico. Her maternal grandfather, Daniel Guzmán, had been a medical doctor who participated in the Mexican Revolution, and her paternal grandfather was Carlos Mastretta, the Italian consul in Puebla during the revolution. Angeles's father was born in Mexico, but he went to Italy as an adolescent; twenty years later he returned to Puebla, where he met and married Angeles's mother. Angeles's father died when she was twenty-one years old, but she still mourns her loss, celebrating Father's Day every day of the year.

Angeles's mother still lives in Puebla, in a house overlooking the volcanoes, and during the summers she takes care of Angeles's

---

[3] See the works cited after Part 4 of this book.
[4] This is my translation, as are all others in this chapter.
[5] See the works cited after part 4 of this book.

children. Of her son and daughter, Angeles declares, "I think that they are both gods and just in case, I venerate them dreadfully" (Mastretta 1992, 20). Angeles is a doting mother, taking pains to explain to her children why they have to eat lunch with us in the middle of a movie they are watching on television. As we eat, she relates the entire plot of the movie to them, using emphatic gestures and repeating the dialogue by memory. Her dramatic reenactment of George Burns's role in *18 Again* entertains us all for the duration of the meal.

Angeles studied journalism in the National Autonomous University of Mexico (UNAM), and in 1974 she received a scholarship from the Mexican Center for Writers. In 1975 her poetry was published with the title *La pájara pinta* (the spotted bird), although the publication was done without her knowledge or permission. In 1985 she received the Mazatlán Literary Prize (*Premio Mazatlán de literatura*) for *Mexican Bolero*. In 1990 she published a collection of short stories, *Mujeres de ojos grandes* (women with big eyes), which by June 1991 had sold more than twenty-three thousand copies. She has published numerous articles in *Nexos* and other cultural magazines, and she has participated as a host on the television talk show *La almohada* (the pillow).

Although Angeles's style is very different from that of Elena Poniatowska, she shares with the other Mexican author a commitment to giving voice to the voiceless. Angeles explained:

> I think that literature in a country like this one is a luxury and therefore it entails a double responsibility. I don't mean that literature should be social propaganda: it wouldn't be any good. What I do believe is that you have a greater responsibility to tell what most people are not going to tell, to recuperate other voices, the voices of people who are not ever going to be able to speak. (Teichmann 519)

Her social commitment is obvious in *Mexican Bolero,* because of the help the main character offers to women of different social and economic classes, and because of Angeles's protagonist, who, because she is a woman, would be relegated to the periphery in traditional Mexican discourse. This novel is an example of the

INTRODUCTION

narrative Molly Hite has analyzed in her book *The Other Side of the Story:*

> In particular, experimental fictions by women seem to share the decentering and disseminating strategies of postmodernist narratives, but they also seem to arrive at these strategies by an entirely different route, which involves emphasizing conventionally marginal characters and themes, in this way recentering the value structure of the narrative. (2)

By focusing on the spouse rather than on the politician, Mastretta has rendered significant a character who otherwise would be overlooked or, at best, secondary. Her narrative reveals how the protagonist struggles to find her own identity and a measure of freedom in a male-dominated society. This story may be read as a serious condemnation of political and sexual oppression, or as a lighthearted love story, and the various translations of the title reflect these disparate interpretations. The title derives from a song by the famous Mexican singer Agustín Lara. The literal translation of the title would be "Tear out My Heart," which would of course emphasize the tragic aspect of the novel. Whereas the German translation (Mexican Tango) also underscores the drama, the English translation (Mexican Bolero) refers to a quick and playful dance that stresses the humor, passion, and fantasy of the novel.

Mujeres de ojos grandes, Angeles's collection of short stories, has both a social and a personal message. Angeles wished to show strong women reacting in unusual ways to difficult situations, but she also wished to entertain her infant daughter as she coaxed her back from the brink of death. She describes how the idea of the book came to her one day in 1985, while she sat next to her three-week-old daughter who was gravely ill:

> I just sat near her one day—once I could talk—and I said, "Look, you can't die, because you have a long line of women behind you. We have all been working a long time for you to be you. So you can't do this to me, and to my aunts, and to

my grandmother, and to everyone. You can't do this. You can't die. I can't have another little girl, so you must live!" And so I began to tell her the story of her aunts. There were so many strong women in my family. I just started telling her that story—of her aunts. And when it was over, I thought to myself, I should write a book about them. (Pedén 89)

This quote reveals Angeles's belief in the healing and transformational potential of narrative. She senses the need to tell stories about strong women, the need to provide alternative narratives for half the world's population, who until recently have been neglected by traditional Mexican narrative. She realizes women need to hear other stories so that we can live other lives, creating alternatives to the worn-out old plots of submission and enclosure. The protagonist of *Mexican Bolero* is confined by her marriage and patriarchal society, but she manages to push against the boundaries of her world and create some freedom for herself within those limits. Many of the women in *Mujeres de ojos grandes* manage to transcend the restrictions imposed on the protagonist of *Mexican Bolero,* but their characters are not adequately developed in the short stories. What we need is what Angeles promises in the following interview: a book-length narrative based on the life of one of the more assertive women in *Mujeres de ojos grandes.*

CHAPTER FIVE

INTERVIEW
ANGELES MASTRETTA

ANGELES MASTRETTA

KG: How and when did you begin to write?[1]
AM: Every time I am asked that, I come up with a different answer. After struggling with doubts, I have discovered that I am a novelist because I love to add details to reality. I don't know, I don't remember when I became a writer. My father was a journalist even though he wasn't paid—he did a thousand other things—and he loved it and I loved my father . . . but besides I have a family that is very apt at telling stories and that has rubbed off on me. Now, as to when I knew that I wanted to write a book, well, I took a long time. First, I studied journalism, but I soon realized that I couldn't be a news writer like other journalists, because I always made up my journalism assignments. We were told, "Do an interview with a politician," and everybody went to interview a local representative and I interviewed the president of the Republic. Then the professor said, "What a prodigious interview! How did you do it?" and I knew that my story was a lie. The same thing happened when we had to write about an accident. My classmates wrote about a simple fender-bender and I told about buses that went over cliffs, and I interviewed the wounded people and the relatives of those who died, and it was all a lie. It was then that I realized that I had to devote my time to inventing, but when I finished college I worked many years as a journalist. Of course I wrote editorials, the kind where you can add details to reality.
KG: How did you get the idea to write *Mexican Bolero?*
AM: I had the idea for a long time, because my second year of college I had a scholarship at the Mexican Center for Writers, so I started a novel, which of course I never finished, but I was left with the idea that I had to write not that novel, but a better one. Then I began to think that the men of power in post-revolutionary Puebla were very attractive. This political boss of whom I speak is one of six men who were very powerful—some of them still are—and they all came out of Puebla: [Gustavo] Díaz Ordaz, who was president of Mexico

---

[1] *This interview took place in August 1991, except for the questions at the end about what she has been writing in the past year, which I asked her in August 1992.*

INTERVIEW

[1964–70]; Gabriel Alarcón, the owner of a newspaper, a credit-card company, and many other things; Manuel Espinoza Iglesias, the former owner of Bancomer [one of the largest banks in Mexico]; William Jenkins, a North American who owned a sugar refinery; and the most attractive character, the governor Maximino Avila Camacho, on whom I based the character in my book. [The sixth man was Maximino's brother, Manuel Avila Camacho, who was president of Mexico from 1940 to 1946.]

I wanted to write a saga in which they all had parts, but I couldn't start out like that, so I chose this one [Maximino Avila Camacho] and I went to Puebla to investigate. Nobody wanted to tell me anything, everybody from his time period lowered their voices when I asked about him. So I thought, well, that's better because I can make things up. I included the few anecdotes that I could find, but I invented the character's personality. How much power did he have? They only told me that he had a lot, I had to guess the extent of it. People said, "He was an assassin," and I had to make up who his victims were because nobody told me who they were.

There was a woman there who was my mother's neighbor, and my mother knew perfectly well that this woman's father had been kidnapped because of a legal battle he had with the governor, and he was killed and cut up into pieces and delivered to his family in a basket. I thought that if that had happened to my father, the only thing that I would want to do would be to talk about that and have somebody publish the story, so I sought out this woman and I invited her to lunch, but she didn't tell me anything. She came with her husband, so he would help her to keep quiet. It was a very frustrating lunch because she was really boring, and all she said was, "I don't know anything."

KG: Do you think that she was still afraid?
AM: I believe so, because she didn't tell me half a word. But she did tell me a very funny story about a woman whom I used as [my protagonist's] friend, a woman who became the lover of her gynecologist. They used to meet in a room above the market, and it was a supersecret piece of gossip in Puebla.

That woman was the grandmother of one of my best friends, and I didn't know anything about it, and neither did my friend. So that woman didn't give me her father's story, but she gave me this other story, and that's how I found some things, and the rest I invented.

KG: What percentage of the novel is fiction?

AM: I believe that the novel is 90 percent fiction, even though I sometimes walked on scaffolding over the real story. For example, I read a lot of history, and I chose 1915 for the year when my character has a first wife, Eulalia. I chose that year because so many things were happening, and I thought it was superattractive to show how 1915 had been for a poor couple. I used everything that I knew about that year, but afterwards I discovered that it was a lie that he had been a milkman then because he was already working for Huerta when Madero was assassinated.[2] When I found that out I said, "How horrible! My story with Eulalia is going to be ruined, I can't use it in my book." And I was frightfully sad because I loved the story with Eulalia. Then I decided that it didn't matter; I would tell it anyway and then say later that he had told that story to his wife but maybe it wasn't true.

KG: You have said that 90 percent of the novel is fiction. What are the historical elements of the novel, the ones that historians should take seriously?

AM: I think that there aren't any. I don't believe that literature should be taken seriously by historians. It should be read for pleasure and enjoyment, but not taken seriously. I think that it would be awful—imagine if you read *Doctor Zhivago* and you believe that it is history, it's the furthest thing from history, even though some stories end up being more important than history. I don't know if the war in *War and Peace* was really like that, but it doesn't matter to me, I believe it was like that, and those are the Russians that I love. When I see now what is happening to the Russians—since I haven't been in Russia—I

---

[2] *Francisco Madero was elected president of Mexico and served from November 1911 to February 1913, when he was shot by the men of Victoriano Huerta, who took over the presidency.*

INTERVIEW

think about them as if they were the characters in *War and Peace*. I suffer for them, I think that there will always be a Natásha and a Prince Andréy, and the other characters from that book.

I think that historians would make a mistake if they accept my book as reality. Perhaps they could use literature as one of their sources—they use thousands—to see how people dressed, how their relationships were, and so forth, but not to find out what a president said or exactly how a governor ran his state. I would say that there are very few things that can be accepted as reality in *Mexican Bolero*.

KG: But can't it offer some commentary or interpretation of history?

AM: I think that [my book] is a rather derogatory comment about politics and life in general in that time period. But at the same time it is an attractive story. I thought that man was terrible, but he did have some agreeable qualities, and he fascinates me; I have a certain weakness for him, for his extravagant personality, like the way he organized expeditions to go from Mexico City to Puebla, deciding which child rode in which car. That was all a lie, but it seemed perfectly believable that a man who was such a scoundrel could manage his family like that, or sit down to drink brandy and play dominoes, and that's why his daughters recognized something of their father in that book. But if they came to me and said, "You're lying about our father," I would say, "Of course I am lying. And what's more, the general in that book is not your father, he is a man that I made up. Now, if you see something of your father there, your father must have been something like that." They haven't said that to me because I don't speak with them, but I have heard that they have said that to others, so there must be something credible about the character for his relatives.

KG: Why did you change the names? Did you want complete freedom to invent?

AM: Of course! Imagine if I hadn't, I would have been accused of being a slanderous liar. I never tried to write history, and it's a good thing that I didn't try because nobody told me anything and the newspapers also didn't reveal anything. All the newspapers glorified the governor, reporting all of his great works, and you could never imagine what he was really like. Even the one short-lived newspaper that criticized his policies didn't butcher him, they only published minicriticisms.

KG: *Mexican Bolero* seems like a diary, because of its confidential tone and its style. Did you plan it like that?

AM: Well, I didn't know how to get into the story, because when I told it in third person, I constantly took pity on the woman and said, "Poor thing, this man took her to such a place." But I couldn't tell it that way; I was frequently giving my opinion, not from her point of view but from mine. It seemed false; I was always judging. So I decided to try a first person, and it was really hard for me to find Catalina's voice, because I don't talk like that. Catalina is very vulgar—she uses slang and bad words—and I am a woman who has been educated to speak in a refined and subtle manner. Perhaps I abused it a little, but I loved to write like that; I found a language that I was happy to use, a language that had not been mine. During those years I was friends with the poet Renato Leduc.[3] He was a fantastic person, full of stories, with an incredible way of talking. I think that Catalina Ascencio speaks like Renato Leduc would have spoken if he had been a woman. Besides, it was essential that Catalina have a sense of humor because her story is so terrible; that story would have been dreadful if it were told without a sense of humor.

KG: Do you think that Catalina is a reliable narrator, or is she exaggerating and making up things?

AM: It depends on how you see her. If you believe that she is a literary character, then she is a reliable narrator; she is telling the whole truth. If you see her as a real person, a historical character, then she is inventing.

KG: Within your fiction, she is telling the truth.

---

[3] *Renato Leduc (1897–1986) was a Mexican poet whose works range from the very early* Los banquetes *(the banquets [1932]) to the more recent* Los diablos del petróleo *(the devils of petroleum [1986]).*

INTERVIEW

AM: Yes, and besides, there is no other truth. What is unique about her is that from the beginning she is undressed, that is, from the first moment, you are inside her and her most illustrious stupidity. What's more, I as a writer could not believe that her lucidity and skill are false. It seems very logical to me, but what happened was that I believed Catalina Ascencio. I think that writers have to believe their characters, or they will write a bad book. Just imagine: the characters that you invent are your partners, your accomplices, they are very much yours. If you don't believe in them, then you can't deal with them, just like you can't deal with real people when you don't believe in them. Why put up with them, unless their lies interest you as literary material, but otherwise, you don't speak to them.

KG: Did you imagine that Catalina was speaking with somebody, or that she was speaking to herself?

AM: I imagined that she was talking to herself. When I began to write, I imagined that she was speaking to somebody like her granddaughter, but that turned out to be very difficult to maintain because it would not have been easy for her to tell her granddaughter all about her extravagant relationship with the governor. Sometimes Catalina is a little anachronistic, because she thinks and even says things like a woman from the eighties. But that's the point, I believe that we women from the eighties are not inventing anything, that all of this has been passing through the heads and the hearts of women for a long time, it just wasn't organized in a massive way, and that's what I propose to show in both this novel and *Mujeres de ojos grandes* (women with big eyes). But these women don't theorize; they react to situations with actions, not with theories.

KG: Why do you suppose Catalina had to poison her husband? Why couldn't she just go far, far away?

AM: I'm not even very sure that she poisoned him. What's more, I believe that she didn't poison him. I think that she believed that she was poisoning him, she tried to play the game that the other woman proposed, but even she knew that she was just playing. I believe that it's very difficult for authors to analyze their own literary characters. You, for example, could probably do a much more convincing analysis of my protagonist than I could. But I believe that Catalina is not capable of killing, not even her husband, because she has a profound sense of humor, and for someone to kill somebody, (s)he has to take things very seriously. I truly believe that in a book of mine a character could only kill somebody who killed her child, and otherwise she would find a way to get rid of that person without having to commit murder; Catalina is a little like that. She knew that she couldn't expect anything else from that man, she knew that he would kill her lover. If she had believed anything else, she would have been a fool, and I don't believe that she was a fool. That's why she gets so angry with her lover, because she supposed that he thought the same way. When he dies, she scolds him, she is furious with him.

KG: Because he has provoked his own death?

AM: Yes. It's very strange because she becomes enraged with her lover rather than with her husband, as if the husband were an element of nature, something irreversible that nobody can oppose. That's why I am not sure that she killed her husband, but she is delighted by his self-destruction as he loses power and doesn't know what to do.

KG: I know that you are concerned about women, since you have written two books about them, but do you consider yourself a feminist?

AM: Actually I think that it's better the way you said it, that I am concerned about women. I'm not sure what it means to be a feminist. If being a feminist means saying that women are very attractive human beings, worthy of our reflections and our research and our fantasies, then I am a feminist. If you tell me that we ought to create a world of women, and that men should be subjugated to us, that they should think and feel just like we do, that would meet with my resistance. I think men are very entertaining. Last week I went to a conference in Quintana Roo, and there were lots of women in the audience. The show was being televised, and there were questions by telephone. Some man called and asked me, "Mrs. Mastretta, do you ever plan to write something profound or do you intend to keep writing about women?" I said, "Look, sir, as long as there are men who ask that kind of question, I ought to keep writing about women so that someone will be concerned with banality, since there probably are many people like you who are very occupied with profound topics." So I think that I can still have the luxury of entertaining myself with women. They are very attractive characters, although in *Mexican Bolero* there are at least two very strong masculine characters.

KG: Do you have a particular message for women?

AM: I don't have messages for anybody. I believe that messages are made for politicians and priests. Writers are only obliged to invent and to tell stories. If the public is moved in some way by what we say, that's great, but we shouldn't give speeches. For me it is a thousand times better to invent a character who does politics than to give a theoretical speech about how women should participate in politics. That's not my job.

KG: But in Mexican literature there are hardly any women who are devoted to politics, or to any other career, or who shape their own destiny in a different way than society has planned.

AM: That's on purpose, that is perfectly deliberate. For me it is much more entertaining to write about the women with big eyes than to tell my own life, even though I have decided who I want to be and I support myself with my career—so what?—I'm not going to tell my story; I don't want to; I bore myself; I already know myself.

Nevertheless, some of the women in *Mujeres de ojos grandes* make their own destiny. There is one who doesn't want to get married; I think she will be my next novel.

KG: In a novel the character would have to have an entirely different scope, a development and complication that she doesn't have in the short story.

AM: Yes, you are right, and that's difficult. For example, I kept writing about Catalina in *Mexican Bolero*. After her husband died, I wrote four more chapters, but I didn't know what to do with her to make her credible. She couldn't just make love with whoever crossed her path; she couldn't become chaste and modest; she couldn't fall passionately in love with anybody; she couldn't start a new business, so what could I do with her? So I decided to just end the book to see what everybody else does with her.

Many feminist critics have asked me why Catalina didn't just spit on her husband and leave. I wasn't writing a feminist thesis, I was writing a story, and it's clear that Catalina wouldn't think of trying to transform Andrés into a supportive husband who changes diapers. That wasn't possible. It would go against the logic of the story if Catalina had tried to convince Andrés to stop being a murderer, to start being a responsible politician and respecting the will of the majority.

KG: Do you think that Mexican women have progressed much in the last twenty years?

AM: Yes, they have progressed a lot. For example, my seven-year-old daughter will never even think of the possibility of not having a career. She is never going to ask herself, "Should I go to the university or not?" That's something that I did, I had to think about it, but she never will. Even girls who are twenty years old now don't ask themselves if they should go to the university or take sewing and cooking classes. They may learn sewing and cooking in addition or as a hobby, but they aren't going to devote themselves to that any more.

KG: But that is in Mexico City. What about in rural areas?

AM: I think that's happening even in rural areas; I think the economic crisis actually helped. For example, this girl who works for me has four nieces between fifteen and eighteen years of age, and they all came from their village. They cut their hair, they save their money, they buy records, they read, and they are going to be different women even though they don't earn a lot of money; at least they aren't going to be beaten by drunken husbands. I think that things are changing.

Now, if you ask me who in my house makes breakfast if the maid isn't here, I do; and who sees that the children wash their faces and go to bed, I do. But that's not going to happen in my daughter's house, not because I gave her a feminist speech, but because she won't be prepared for that; she didn't grow up that way. I have that hope. . . .

KG: What people and events have influenced your literary work?

AM: I think that my father influenced my literary work, as

INTERVIEW

well as my maternal grandfather, a crazy uncle of mine who built sailboats, Stendhal, García Márquez, Renato Leduc, Jaime Sabines and Martín Luis Guzmán.[4]

KG: And Carlos Fuentes?[5]

AM: I am reading Fuentes now, after having become his friend, but I never read Fuentes when I was young. I think that he is a strong presence in everyone's life, but I think that Elena Poniatowska and Elena Garro[6] weigh on me more.

KG: What about the student movement of 1968 or the economic crisis of the 1980s?

AM: In 1968 I still lived in Puebla, and the newspapers were censured, so I didn't even find out that there had been a student movement until 1971, when I entered the university. So I can't tell you that I carried picket signs, or anything like that, why should I make up a history that I don't have? I have the history of a girl who did embroidery in Puebla, the extraordinary thing is that I'm not still doing embroidery in Puebla. For me the breakthrough was when I left Puebla, a city that still resembled the Puebla of *Mujeres de ojos grandes,* and I entered a place where the [disaster of] '68 had happened. It was an incredible leap. For me, entering the national university was like going to five Disneylands at once, everything was marvelous, everything was fun. Then four months after I

---

[4]*Stendhal was the pen name used by the French author Henri Beyle (1783–1842), who was best known for his book* Le Rouge et le Noir *(The Red and the Black). The Columbian author Gabriel García Márquez (1928–) is best known for his Nobel Prize–winning novel* One Hundred Years of Solitude. *The Mexican poet Jaime Sabines (1926–) has published* Crónicas del volcán *(chronicles of the volcano [1988]) and* En mis labios te sé *(on my lips I know you [1961]), as well as his collected works. Martín Luis Guzmán (1887–1976) was known for his novels on the Mexican Revolution, including* El águila y la serpiente *(The Eagle and the Serpent) and* La sombra del caudillo *(the shadow of the leader).*

[5]*Carlos Fuentes (1928–) is a well-known Mexican author whose translated works include* The Death of Artemio Cruz, Terra Nostra, *and* Christopher Unborn.

[6]*The Mexican author Elena Garro (1920–) is best known for her first novel, translated as* Recollections of Things to Come. *She is mentioned in the next part as an influence on Silvia Molina, also.*

started classes, my father died, and I was left without any money. I had to work to go to the university, just like everybody else. What would have been dreadful in a private university—where everybody has fathers and mothers and cars and chauffeurs and everything—was wonderful in a public university because it made me like everybody else. I became close friends with people with whom I had never associated before, and that was very enriching, very gratifying; I learned to speak differently, and to think differently.

KG: What was it that kept you from staying in Puebla, doing embroidery?

AM: I'm not sure if it was destiny or good luck. Probably good luck. I was very restless, very curious, even though I have become lazy now. My children have become an anchor, but that doesn't bother me. They amuse me a lot, they attract me, and I believe that mothers should accompany their children as they grow. I can't shoo them away when I'm working. In contrast, my husband feels that it's perfectly logical to tell them to go away and not come back for three months, but I can't do that. That's my own whirlwind, and I don't plan to change that whirlwind.

KG: How do you combine being a wife and mother with being a writer?

AM: Very poorly. I combine [those duties] however I can. I always get interrupted to deal with things in the kitchen, and then I have a hard time concentrating again. I have a burn here because of stewing over feminist theses in the kitchen. My husband and I were chatting with a friend, and he said to me, "Why don't you bring us some coffee?" So I went to make them coffee. Then when I had the coffee ready, I thought, "Why am I serving this coffee?" And instead of concentrating on serving it, I poured it on my hand. Because of arguing with myself, I served coffee on my hand. It's better to argue anywhere but the kitchen.

Now, I like to cook; it is embroidery I never liked. I am never going to teach my daughter to do embroidery. She will sew on a button, but never do embroidery.

KG: What was the purpose of *Mujeres de ojos grandes?*

INTERVIEW

AM: I proposed to tell many different stories about common, ordinary women, conservative and traditional, who suddenly had something unusual happen to them and they responded in an unusual way. They didn't respond like other people in their time period; they responded with joy instead of sadness, or with a sense of humor, or with bravery. They did things that nobody—not even the women themselves—expected of them. For example, when one woman receives a marriage proposal, she doesn't want to get married; and another finds out that her husband has a lover, so she reveals that she has a lover, too. Then there are two sisters who are very close, and one is dying of cancer. Rather than hide their feelings, they talk about their sadness and their rage because they are losing each other. And that's the point, they don't pretend. When I was young, especially when my father died, everybody said that it was laudable not to cry. I didn't want to behave myself and gracefully receive visitors when my father died. I wanted to howl, and everybody would have thought I was crazy. The people who repress their emotions are the ones who are crazy, not I. And these two sisters realize that. As I told these stories, I was trying to mix irony and intelligence, as a way of redeeming people from mediocrity.

KG: Why big eyes? Do they symbolize something?

AM: Yes, they see further than others. They are in a place where everybody has the same horizon, but they see beyond the common horizon.

KG: And do they want to achieve something more, or just see?

AM: Since they are capable of seeing further, then they are also more capable of acting as a consequence of what they see. For example, one of the women has a husband who has a lover. When the husband gets sick, the wife takes him to the lover, instead of keeping him to herself. She sees that the lover is the only one who can share her pain. She is an extravagant woman, even for this time period. That was the point, to show unusual women.

KG: Do you have a routine for writing?

AM: Yes, I have a schedule, which is more and more abused. When my children are in school, I have a regular schedule; I write from nine to three, because when they come home it's over. Now that they are in Puebla [for summer vacation], I can chat in the morning and work in the afternoon, which is when I concentrate better.

KG: Do you sometimes collaborate with your husband?

AM: Well, I write for the magazine that he directs [*Nexos* (connections)], which was hard for me to accept at first. Now I take it for granted. I am envious of him, though, because he goes to his study and says, "Everybody be quiet," and then he just shuts out the world. Of course, while he writes a seven-hundred-page novel, I take care of the children and struggle with two pages. It doesn't bother me any more, though. Each one has his own luck; while he has all that time to write, I have written a very successful book. We work very well together.

KG: Is there rivalry between you two?

AM: I think that there was, but only on my part, because he doesn't mind at all if I tell him that I'm going to Sweden, he thinks that's fine. He never complains that I wrote a book that is more famous than his. So I decided not to feel rivalry, either; we are actually good friends.

KG: What would you like to do, besides writing?

AM: I would like to have been a singer. I always sing around the house—ta ra ra [she sings]—I spend the day singing, and I am envious of all singers, even the bad ones.

KG: What have you been writing this past year [1992]?

AM: This past year I have been writing brief literary articles for my column "Puerto Libre" (free port) in the magazine *Nexos*. The themes come from within, and they break with the general tone of the magazine because the whole magazine is usually turned outward, toward society, and I am writing texts that turn inward; they enter a personal, intimate world. For example, I wrote about my father and the pain that I still feel more than twenty years after his death. I really like to write these articles, but I think that they have stolen my energy; they have robbed me of the creativity that I need to put in my next book.

KG: What can you tell me about your next book?

INTERVIEW

AM: My next book is not even in the oven yet, I am just buying the ingredients. I am beginning to decide who my character will be: she will be a woman born in 1890 or 1900, and she will be like the aunts in *Mujeres de ojos grandes,* but I want a long look at her life, not just a glimpse. But when I finally manage to write three lines, somebody calls on the phone or the plumber arrives or the electrician is here and somebody needs money to go buy tomatoes and they ask me a hundred questions about the midday meal.... Living with such a multiplicity of demands is a challenge that I suppose we women all have; you have to manage to concentrate on several things at once so you don't lose your place or your passion for what you are doing.

[My protagonist] will work in a pharmacy in Puebla, selling medicine, and at the same time she will become a folk-healer (*curandera*). She will be a good listener and she will help people get out of depressions, for example, people who would otherwise end up in an insane asylum. The idea that somebody can be depressed but not crazy is a concept of the eighties, but I want to put it in the head of a woman of the twenties or thirties. I want her to discover, perhaps through intuition, things that are considered perfectly natural in the eighties. So, this woman has a relationship with an adventurer, and she goes off on trips with him, but she always wants to come back. And I know that the feminists are going to say, "Why is the woman the sedentary one? Why can't she be the adventurer?" But I don't want to think about what they are going to ask me, I just want to write my book the way I feel it. And it feels right to have the woman be the sedentary one, perhaps because I have a tendency to be sedentary. Anyway, he is a compulsive traveler—he has infinite curiosity about the world—and she is torn between wanting to go with him and her own passion for the people she needs around her.

KG: Do you know how you will resolve her dilemma?

AM: No, of course I don't know. I suppose I will resolve it by not resolving it; that is, I suppose I will allow time to make him more sedentary.

KG: Perhaps she will become more adventurous as he becomes more sedentary.

AM: Probably. And of course she will have all sorts of adventures all over the world because they will travel a lot. And there will be difficulties putting this all in the past, because I will have to know how they traveled to Vienna, for example, what the boat looked like, and what Vienna was like before World War II. [For the pharmacy scenes I need to know] what medicines were sold, and what cream they used on their faces. All of that is a big challenge not only to my imagination but also to my research abilities. People tell me to write it in the present, but it would lose half the fascination for me if I moved it to the present.

KG: Do you have another project in mind?

AM: I have a story that is pending, the story of my father. In the July *Nexos* my column is about my father, who is an obsession in my life; he is a ghost who haunts me, and it would be a magnificent challenge to write about the part of his life that is completely unknown to me. My father was Mexican, but my grandfather was Italian, and he sent my father to Italy and [my father] didn't come back for twenty years. During those twenty years he went from being fourteen years old to being thirty-four, he went through the Second World War, he was educated, and many other things happened that he never mentioned. My mother doesn't know what he did during those years. So I said to her, "How is it possible to sleep with a man for twenty years, and not know what he did during the preceding twenty years?" But my mother is not like I am, so she didn't ask. That is a precious story, a fascinating story that attracts me very much, but it is also very painful. So I don't know if I want to rescue that story right now or not. All that I can offer you right now is doubts.

KG: What advice would you give a writer who is just beginning her career?

AM: That she not pay attention to others, because that is completely absurd. I don't mean that she shouldn't read other books or that she shouldn't love other writers, but she shouldn't try to create the way others do because that can be fatal. She shouldn't feel obliged to follow any style other than her own, and she should be very demanding with her own

INTERVIEW

work; she should reread it many times, and make corrections. I always read my work many times and make many changes, until I turn in the manuscript. Then I leave it alone and don't read it any more. Also, she should have friends who are good readers: not friends who say, "This is precious," but friends who say, "This isn't right. If I were you, I wouldn't resolve it this way." The readers can't tell you how it should be, but they can tell you when it's wrong. And I'm not going to give you any more advice because [my husband] Hector has arrived.

CHAPTER SIX

Fidelity, Credibility, and Duplicity in Angeles Mastretta's *Mexican Bolero*

Lord Peter Wimsey once said
that nine-tenths
of the law of chivalry
was a desire to have
all the fun.
The same might well
be said of patriarchy.

CAROLYN HEILBRUN,
WRITING A WOMAN'S LIFE

LENA PONIATOWSKA'S *MASSACRE IN MEXICO* AND *NADA, NADIE* (nothing, nobody) subvert the official story as told by political speeches and news releases, by presenting innumerable eyewitness accounts of the government's actions. A contrast is established between what the PRI[1] officials said in the fateful years of 1968 and 1985, and what they actually did. This same subversive process is evident in Mastretta's *Mexican Bolero*.[2] Although Poniatowska's work is nonfiction and Mastretta's book is a novel, the same ironic contrast between official words and governmental actions is presented in both texts. Because of her journalistic approach, however, Poniatowska has chosen to record only verifiable facts and events actually witnessed by people willing to testify. In contrast, Mastretta's fictional mode gives her the freedom to use anonymous testimony and follow up on rumors and speculation, while remaining free from censorship or charges of libel. This points out a second irony in Mastretta's text, the possibility of revealing truth through fiction.

Manipulation of history is a common problem throughout Latin America, and contemporary writers often circumvent censorship and contradict official interpretations by writing short stories and novels. Fiction thus becomes a valuable means of communication about social and political reality, as Mastretta demonstrates with her novel. Set in Puebla in the 1930s, *Mexican Bolero* tells the story of a woman who married into one of the most powerful families in Mexico. The text is based on the

---

[1] The PRI is the Institutionalized Revolutionary party, the ruling political party in Mexico since 1929 (with two name changes). For a thorough discussion of the PRI's strong-arm tactics, see part 1, chapter 3, of this book.
[2] For the convenience of my English-speaking audience, all page numbers are from the English version of *Arráncame la vida*, which is: *Mexican Bolero*, trans. Ann Wright (London: Viking, 1989).

ANGELES MASTRETTA

life of Margarita Richardi, the wife of Maximino Avila Camacho,[3] and it reveals her struggle for integrity and independence.

The author does not pretend to have written a history book. An important distinction can be made between fiction and nonfiction. Nonfiction works are referential texts, subject to the test of verification outside of the text (Lejeune 211). The resemblance of a text to an external reality is called *exactitude*, and it concerns information, whereas *fidelity* is a reflection of the meaning or spirit of a given period (Lejeune 211). Fiction is more often concerned with fidelity; nonfiction aspires to exactitude.

Even though *Mexican Bolero* lacks exactitude, because names and details are changed, it does appear to have a high degree of fidelity to the political situation of that time. The novel also has inherent credibility, derived from the authority of the narrator as a politician's wife, who offers a first-person, eye-witness account of the action behind the scenes. Her point of view is dead center, which narrows the distance between herself and what she narrates. She proves to be a reliable narrator, consistent with her own testimony and actions, and the words and deeds of other characters confirm her descriptions.

Andrés Ascencio, the narrator's husband, is obviously a fictional portrayal of Maximino Avila Camacho, governor of the state of Puebla from 1937 to 1941. There are numerous examples of correspondence between the lives of Avila Camacho and Ascencio: their appointment as military commander of Puebla in 1935, their alliance with President Lázaro Cárdenas (1934–40), their friendship with the North American entrepreneur William Jenkins, and the arranged marriages of their daughters to rich members of the community.[4] In spite of these similari-

---

[3]*Maximino Avila Camacho was a member of a very influential family; one brother, Manuel, served as Mexico's president from 1940 to 1946, and another brother, Rafael, served as governor of Puebla from 1951 to 1957. Besides being governor of Puebla for one term, Maximino served in the cabinet of his brother Manuel.*

[4]*Wil Pansters, in Politics and Power in Puebla, asserts in a footnote: "The image of the 'ruthless macho' is excellently described by Angeles Mastretta in her novel Arráncame la vida . . . , based on the life of Maximino's wife Margarita Richardi" (183 n. 9). When he discusses the cooperation between Avila Camacho and William Jenkins, Pansters refers to the novel again: "For a fictionalized version of these events see Mastretta's Arráncame la vida" (184 n. 39).*

ties, the novel does not aspire to historical accuracy, as the changes of names and details would indicate, and thus is more concerned with fidelity than exactitude.

Nevertheless, the reader's acceptance of the fidelity of the text depends in part on the similarities between fact and fiction; it also depends on the diminished aesthetic distance between the narrator and the reader. This distance is reduced by the fact that the protagonist of *Mexican Bolero*, Catalina Guzmán, is a *limited narrator*, to borrow Wayne Booth's term and definition, who offers a realistic version of events that could be observed by only one person (102). Catalina does not present herself as a narrator, nor does she refer to the narrating process. She makes no attempt to explain the motive for her narrative. She also does not establish an "epic situation," as defined by Bertil Romberg; that is, she does not define her position in time and space and, consequently, the distance between the plane of narration and the plane of action, called *Erzähldistanz,* is not explicit (Romberg 96–97). Telling her story in chronological order, Catalina matures and develops as she narrates. She is, therefore, what Dorrit Cohn labels a consonant self-narrator, one who is an "unobtrusive narrator who identifies with his earlier incarnation, renouncing all manner of cognitive privilege" (155). The key word in Cohn's definition is *unobtrusive.* In other words, Catalina does not create distance between herself and her narrated self.

Mastretta's novel, however, is not what Romberg would call a "perfect fictional memoir," that is, one in which the author does not enter at all (38–39). Besides the conscious or direct information that the narrator reveals about herself, there is some unconscious information that the author communicates indirectly to the reader. The author and the reader meet over the narrator's head. Although the narrator makes no apologies or justification for her actions, and she seems to take for granted that anyone would do the same as she has, some criticism is implied by the author in regard to Catalina's addiction to material luxuries, her avoidance of knowledge of Andrés's corruption, and her inability to leave or stand up to her husband.

Catalina's credibility as a narrator is closely linked to her intellectual development. The impression of fidelity that is conveyed by the novel is enhanced because the reader is allowed to witness the narrator's personal and political awakening. When Catalina first meets Andrés, she is fifteen years old and he is over thirty. He immediately goads her to agree with him, without explaining about what:

> Suddenly he put his hand on my shoulder and said, "They're such idiots, aren't they?"
> I looked around, not knowing what to say.
> "Who?" I asked.
> "Say yes, your face says you agree," he said, laughing.
> I said yes, but again asked who.
> He had green eyes and, winking one of them, said, "Puebla people, sweetie. Who else?" (3)

Catalina is aware of Andrés's attitude toward her; he treats her like a child who can be bullied and derided into agreeing with him. However, by asking again who, she reveals a seed of personal awakening, and her own stubborn insistence that she be recognized as a separate individual. The narrator keeps her ears open, and soon she has learned enough to express her opinion, even though it is still met with derision:

> He called [his political rival] a fool, but worried about him as though he weren't.
> "He can't be such a fool if you're so concerned about him," I said one afternoon. We were watching the sunset.
> "Of course he's a fool. What business is it of yours, anyway? Who asked your opinion?"
> "You've been talking about the same old thing for four days, time enough for me to have an opinion."
> "Hark at the lady. She doesn't know how babies are made, yet she already wants to boss generals around. I'm getting to like her," he said. (7)

In spite of her obvious intelligence, Catalina has little more than an elementary education, and once she marries Andrés she settles into the traditional roles of housewife and mother. Nonetheless, when Andrés becomes a candidate for governor of Puebla, they move into an enormous mansion and Catalina finds herself supervising forty servants and administering the money required to feed fifty to three hundred guests a day. Soon after his election, Andrés names his wife the president of the Charity Board, putting her in charge of the insane asylum, the orphanage, and various hospitals.

Even though Catalina takes these duties seriously and succeeds in improving conditions in the institutions, she is not given the respect that she deserves. "For most people I was part of the furniture," she complains, "someone you paid as much attention to as you would a chair that sat at [the] table and smiled" (62).

When Catalina protests the killing of twelve Indians by the Army, her husband dismisses her concerns as those of a mere woman: " 'That's just like a woman. You were talking about her intelligence and then she goes all sentimental,' said Andrés" (91). Her husband is continuously hushing her, and he even states that she can't know anything more than what he tells her, thus claiming total domination of her cognitive functions as well as her actions.

The narrator struggles to resist Andrés's efforts to control her: she manages to learn how to drive without his knowledge, and she reads the newspapers to find out about everything that Andrés claims is none of her business. Eventually she is able to have male friends, but Andrés chooses the first one because he is a homosexual and poses no threat to Andrés. Later on Catalina finds herself a lover, but Andrés has him killed. After a brief mourning period, Catalina resigns herself to her fate and reconciles with Andrés, who has the power to open or close doors for her. When he finishes his term as governor and they move to Mexico City, she discovers that she no longer has official duties and for a short time she is stuck in the house. It is Andrés who arbitrarily ends her isolation:

> "From now on you're coming with me everywhere. Your confinement is over," [said Andrés].
> No sooner said than done, because he wished it so, because he was like that. He ebbed and flowed like the bloody sea. And that day he decided to flow. (132)

Catalina is only allowed out of her house during the day, and she is usually accompanied by her husband. Only Andrés can go out alone at night; the house is always guarded by a group of taciturn men who are forbidden to talk to anybody, and who only say, "I'm sorry, you can't go any further" (62). The narrator tries to escape, getting on a bus to another town, but she is overwhelmed by the uncertainty of her "new life" and she returns immediately. She reveals her own lack of identity, and her inability to live apart from Andrés:

> I preferred not to know what Andrés did. I was the mother of his children, the lady of his house, his wife, his maid, his habit, his joke. Who knows what I was, but whatever it was I had to go on being it—however much I sometimes wanted to escape to a country where I didn't exist. (61)

Her failed attempt to escape exposes a basic weakness in the narrator's character: she is intelligent enough to run the Charity Board and the governor's mansion, and to write Andrés's speeches, yet she is not strong enough to face life on her own, separate from Andrés. As previously noted, the author at times communicates something to the reader that the narrator does not consciously acknowledge. On more than one occasion, the author implies that Catalina's dependence on material luxuries is one reason for her inability to escape. For example, Catalina mentions her ninety pairs of shoes, not with any sense of guilt, but rather in the context of not being able to find the ones she wants. And the reader can almost imagine the author winking when the narrator explains her choice of furs with childlike naïveté: "I had on a fox fur. The most beautiful coat I ever had. Furs can be vulgar, but I wore this fox with boots and felt like a Hollywood star" (132).

Thus, although there is very little distance between the plane of narration and the plane of action, the reader may perceive some distance between the author and the narrator. This distance is evident as the narrator conceives of and supposedly attempts to carry out her plan to poison her husband gradually by serving him black-lemon tea every day. Actually, she may not have poisoned him. Catalina may have deluded herself into think-

FIDELITY, CREDIBILITY, AND DUPLICITY

ing that she was poisoning him, and perhaps his death is attributable to natural causes or to his decadent life-style. Nevertheless, most readers believe that Catalina poisoned her husband. But Mastretta's claim that Catalina didn't kill him reveals a deep ambivalence toward her protagonist's intentions and actions. Even though Mastretta acknowledges Catalina's desire to get rid of Andrés, the author can not openly condone such a radical—and ultimately cowardly—act as surreptitious murder. She also would not be content to leave her character as a passive victim, and it would not be credible for Catalina to leave Andrés and embark upon a new life. Mastretta has resolved this dilemma by means of ambiguity: the reader is the ultimate judge of Catalina's character and actions.

Whether the source of the poison is interior or exterior, Andrés eventually does die, and his death represents the end of the old *macho* order. Catalina is finally set free by widowhood, the ideal state for a woman, according to what she is told at her husband's wake. "You bury your dead husband," an experienced widow tells her, "you honour his memory whenever necessary, and then get on with all the things you couldn't do when he was alive" (260). After the funeral, Catalina ponders:

> I wanted to feel the grief of never seeing him again. I couldn't. I felt free. I was afraid. . . . There were so many things I would never have to do again. I was myself, nobody could order me about. So many things I could do, I thought laughing to myself in the pouring rain. Sitting on the ground, playing with the wet earth around Andrés's grave. Delighted with my future, almost happy. (267–68)

The narrator seems to be talking to herself about events that are still quite vivid in her mind. Her narrative resembles a mental diary, one that could never be discovered or unlocked, and she is therefore unconcerned about being misunderstood or judged. The result is that the reader believes her, in spite of—or maybe even because of—the occasional distance between the author and the narrator. Catalina is very credible since she has no motive to lie, even though she would rather not face some of the truths that she reveals, and her reliability enhances the impression of fidelity that the novel conveys.

Her husband, on the contrary, has ample motivation to lie, and one of the most powerful aspects of the novel is the unmasking of the governor of Puebla. The first indication of Andrés's hypocritical nature occurs on the physical plane, as Catalina describes him: "He had large hands and lips that inspired fear when pressed together and confidence when they laughed. It was as though he had two mouths" (3).

This clue proves reliable, as the narrator reveals time and time again the contrast between what Andrés *says* (about his youth as a Maderista,[5] his profamily stance, his lament for the deaths of his opponents, and his call for justice) and what Andrés *does* (he was actually a Huertista, he abused his own family, he ordered the deaths of many who opposed him, and he obstructed justice). This contrast between words and deeds is established by means of the discourse/counter-discourse technique discussed in chapter 3. Andrés's words are quoted, and then they are contradicted by the narrator. Besides being a biography of a politician's wife, the text thus becomes an antibiography of a politician; in other words, it subverts the official history of a public figure. This subversion is particularly important when one considers the extraordinary power exercised by the PRI over the Mexican media, and the official party's ability to create whitewashed images of their leaders.

Shortly after the birth of their first child, Andrés tells Catalina a long, romantic story about his youth in Mexico City, when he delivered milk with his first wife, Eulalia, and supported Madero's revolutionary efforts. The narrator believes this tall tale until a document arrives at their house, revealing that Andrés was actually under the orders of the antirevolutionary Huerta.[6] The politician's lies about his idealistic past are thus exposed.

---

[5] *Francisco I. Madero initiated the Mexican Revolution of 1910 that overthrew the dictatorship of Porfirio Díaz. Madero was president of Mexico from 1911 to 1913, when he was overthrown by General Victoriano Huerta, who brought back many of Porfirio Díaz's dictatorial policies. Huerta was president from 1913 to 1914.*

[6] *Wil Pansters mentions that very little is known about Maximino Avila Camacho's military career, but he was believed to be just another Artemio Cruz (the protagonist in Carlos Fuentes' novel* The Death of Artemio Cruz, *who represents an opportunistic sell-out to the U.S. interests).*

FIDELITY, CREDIBILITY, AND DUPLICITY

During Andrés's campaign for governor, he makes a strong pitch for the unity and sanctity of the family. In Coetzalan, Andrés's daughters and Catalina adorn themselves with indigenous dresses and parade through the town, attracting people to Andrés's speech. He takes advantage of the situation and introduces them: "People of Coetzalan. This is my family, a family just like yours, simple and united. Our families are the most precious things we have and I promise you that my government will work to give them the future they deserve" (49).

Catalina listens politely to this pious proclamation, as she stands next to Andrés's illegitimate children, some of whom have been forcefully separated from their mothers. In another speech Andrés declares that Mexican women should unite to defend the rights of female workers and peasants, as well as their equal rights in marriage. The narrator comments:

> From then on I never believed a single speech he made. Worse still, three days later he spoke with ardent passion about the experience of communal land-owning and that very same afternoon he drank a toast with Heiss to celebrate the deal that gave him back the farms expropriated under the Nationalization Law. He told so many lies that once at a meeting in the bullring, people got justifiably angry and set fire to [the bullring]. (48)

In this quotation Catalina is referring to the United States honorary consul, Michael Heiss, whose real name outside of the novel was William Jenkins, and whose immense fortune derived from an alleged kidnapping hoax and the expropriation of peasants' land, with help from the governor of Puebla.[7]

In a political speech on 1 May 1937, Maximino Avila Camacho set himself up as "guardian of the masses": "So we Mexican revolutionaries have learned the need to organize the government in such a way that the state always acts as the guardian of the masses" (Pansters 73). In the novel, Catalina learns that Andrés had more

---

[7]David Ronfeldt describes William Jenkins's accumulation of wealth and power in Puebla in his book Atencingo: The Politics of Agrarian Struggle in a Mexican Ejido.

than twenty striking workers killed, and that he had also ordered the massacre of the peasants who were claiming land in Atencingo. Andrés informs the press: "A very unfortunate thing to have happened . . . I have asked the public prosecutor to investigate the matter thoroughly and I can assure you justice will be done" (80).

Andrés also promises justice in the case of the disappearance of the director of *Avante,* the only local newspaper critical of his policies. Catalina, who suspects Andrés of ordering the journalist's death, witnesses Andrés's interview with the representative of a major Mexican newspaper, *Excélsior.* Andrés assured him that he had requested the intervention of the national Senate, and that he would personally see that justice was done. Pansters also comments on this incident:

> Another critical journalist, José Trinidad Mata, director of the weekly magazine *Avante,* was killed in 1939. Although Maximino was generally considered the brain behind the murder and was sharply criticized by the national press, his political contacts in Mexico City kept him from being prosecuted. (64)

In the novel, Andrés also is implicated in the death of Javier Uriarte, his daughter's boyfriend. Andrés wanted his daughter to marry the son of a wealthy Puebla man in order to cement his relations with the city's upper class. A year after her boyfriend's mysterious death, she complies.

Andrés is ironically eloquent at the funeral of Catalina's lover, whose death he had ordered:

> Carlos Vives was a victim of those who want to prevent our society from marching forward along the fruitful paths of peace and harmony. We do not know who cut short his life, the beautiful life they saw as such a danger, but rest assured that they will pay for their crime. The loss of a man like Carlos Vives not only brings grief to those like myself, my family and his friends who had the privilege of loving him, it is also an irreparable loss to society. (207–8)

FIDELITY, CREDIBILITY, AND DUPLICITY

After the funeral, Andrés and all of his political allies make official statements to the police. According to Catalina, they all agree that Carlos had been a great man, that his death must be avenged, the assassins must be found, and the country must be saved from the threat of violence. The police chief Pellico is accused of the murder, but before he enters prison he comes to visit Andrés. A few months later Pellico is allowed to escape from prison, and for years he sends Christmas cards to Andrés and Catalina from Los Angeles.

The narrator thus establishes the blatant difference between what Andrés says and what he does, offering his speeches as the official discourse and her negation of his words as the counter-discourse. She also tries to create for herself an alternative discourse, her own story, told from her marginalized position within Mexican politics and society. This story is enhanced by the impression of believability and fidelity to the time period, the lack of aesthetic distance, the correspondence between fictitious and actual people and events, and the confirmation of bits and pieces of Catalina's version of events that can be found in the historical record. The narrator is speaking to herself; she has no external addressee, so she is ultimately truthful, in spite of the fact that part of her would rather not face the truth. Mastretta, however, does have addressees—her reading public—and therefore she has chosen to be somewhat duplicitous. She tells Catalina's story in words that she has appropriated from men. As Mastretta has said, Catalina speaks like Renato Leduc would have spoken if he had been a woman.[8] In *Women Writing about Men*, Jane Miller refers to women's acquisition of "masculine" language as a form of bilingualism, an asset with hidden hazards:

> Bilingualism can be an asset . . . , but its acquisition involves splits and instabilities, impersonation, a stepping out of yourself. We can expect double vision and shifting ground in the novels of women. We shall need to hold the notions of dividedness,

---

[8]*Some of the color and piquancy of the narrator's language is unfortunately lost in translation. The Spanish language has an incredible diversity of expressions that can only be translated by one worn-out, obscene word in English.*

even as we consider the more straightforward ways in which women have written about men. (17)

Miller explains that bilingualism is a female strategy for survival, necessary because men are our "first and most dangerous enemy, as well as the first and most desired of allies" (248). Thus, the point of view in *Mexican Bolero* is that of a woman, but the language and even the plot is principally that of a man. Catalina is the wife of a governor, not the politician herself, and when that subordination ends, the narrative stops, because—as Mastretta admitted in our interview—there is nothing for Catalina to do that would be both credible and captivating. The romance plot cannot suddenly be transformed into a quest plot.[9] Mastretta has disguised her message of rebellion as a love story with a traditional plot; criticism of the patriarchal system in Mexican families and government has been embedded within an extravagant and engaging fantasy. Just as Mastretta wears makeup, she says, so as not to offend people, she applies linguistic and narrative cosmetics to her story so as not to insult the Mexican elite. Janet N. Gold has identified Mastretta's narrative as duplicitous and complicitous, because "sometimes the message of rebellion is explicit, concealing a level of complicity; at other times a stated complicity is the mask for a barely concealed rebellion" (1988, 36). In other words, when Catalina declares that she is rebelling, she is actually covering up her concession to Andrés's power; when she pretends to comply with his demands, she is rebelling in secret. Gold concludes that this duplicity is a strategy for success: "By so successfully entering into the Mexican publishing world, Angeles Mastretta has, like her fictional protagonist Catalina Guzmán de Ascencio, created a liberated space from which to extend the boundaries of rebellion" (40).

Miller, also, does not present bilingual duplicity in a negative way. Rather, she points out the progress being made:

> Slowly things are changing. We begin to recognize one another, to winnow out evidence of secret resistances and

---

[9] Traditional romance and quest plots are discussed in Rachel Blau DuPlessis's *Writing Beyond the Ending*.

FIDELITY, CREDIBILITY, AND DUPLICITY

> invasions. Sometimes those secret and coded signals are more exciting than the boldest declarations of mutiny, for they alert us to the kinds of accommodation women have made to their subordination and to the privacies and the powers they have snatched for themselves. We can begin to understand what they have made of the myths and stories which reduce them and which they retell with subtle differences. It has so often been in their own interests for women to accept, or seem to accept, the constraints put on them, as due to their natural inferiority, that they have not found it easy to deny the part they have played themselves in maintaining those determinations, which they have felt as oppressive and yet needed to welcome as inevitable and secure. (28–29)

Mastretta's "secret and coded signals" are exciting, and remarkable. She has appropriated masculine language and the traditional romance plot, and transformed them in order to transmit a strong criticism of regional and national politicians and a scathing commentary on the Mexican macho's attitude toward women. Within her "masculine" discourse, she creates an alternative discourse that gives a voice to women and challenges the official story.

Mastretta's narrative is, therefore, both complicitous and duplicitous, as Gold suggests. The reliable narrator could be compared to a "mole," one of those agents sent out by an intelligence agency to live undercover in a community for a long time, establishing credibility and then funneling information back to be used by the duplicitous agency. The same cooperation may be said to exist between the reliable narrator and the duplicitous author of *Mexican Bolero*.

The novel's complexities do not end here. Catalina, however reliable she is as a narrator, is a complicated and contradictory character. She is duplicitous with Andrés so that she can manipulate him and do as she pleases, and she is hypocritical with the people of Puebla, as she plays the part of the good governor's wife. She would like to delude herself, too—by avoiding knowledge of Andrés's actions and thus denying her complicity—but she isn't quite capable of lying to herself (which is why she is a reliable narrator). Catalina is not a female hero, that is, a woman who takes an active role in shaping her life (Heilbrun

1972, 47). Instead, she endures her degrading situation, pretending that she is getting revenge or—if the reader believes that she poisoned Andrés—actually committing a cowardly act. She is aware of Andrés's hypocrisy, but she nevertheless stands by him and helps him consolidate power, thus contributing to her own oppression and to that of others. *Mexican Bolero* therefore implies another criticism: that of the submissive woman who acquiesces to machismo, out of fear, a lack of preparation for a career, and a need for security. We might see in this final criticism a hint of Mastretta's self-mocking, as she reveals her contradictory attitude toward her own successful accommodation within the Mexican political and familial systems. Mastretta's ironic sense of humor is most endearing when aimed at herself, for it diminishes the distance between her narrator and herself, and between the author and the reader, because to one degree or another, everyone is guilty of accommodation. Nonetheless, Mastretta does not dwell on guilt. She tells this story with a delightful flair, and if she is duplicitous, she is so in a theatrical way: she puts on the mask of drama, and entertains her public. Her play-acting is a game, whose energy and enthusiasm reflect her own fun-loving attitude toward life and writing, and thus she reaches a wider audience than she would have if she had written an unmasked tirade against oppression.

Mastretta's principal achievement in this novel is having presented the life of a woman whose story would traditionally be suppressed. Carolyn Heilbrun, in *Writing a Woman's Life,* has lamented the lack of interaction among women, and our inability to communicate profoundly with each other. Women need to hear and to talk to each other in order to create new narratives, as she explains:

> As long as women are isolated one from the other, not allowed to offer other women the most personal accounts of their lives, they will not be part of any narrative of their own. Like Penelope awaiting Ulysses, weaving and unweaving, women will be staving off destiny and not inviting or inventing or controlling it. They will live their lives individually, among the suitors, without a story to be told, wondering whether

or when to marry.... There will be narratives of female lives only when women no longer live their lives isolated in the houses and the stories of men. (46–47)

Mastretta has made narrative progress by communicating the life of a rebellious woman, even though that woman is still locked in a man's house and in a man's story. Another major stride is taken by Silvia Molina in her novel *La familia vino del norte* (the family came from the north), because she presents a female protagonist who evades the traditional romance plot by refusing to accept a man's interpretation of her life and of her family's history. Molina's protagonist resists the temptation to marry and to fit into her boyfriend's and her family's traditional plans for her; thus she becomes a female hero and writes a story of her own. Mastretta has created a nontraditional narrator; Molina pushes a little further, and creates a protagonist who is both a narrator and an author.

PART III
SILVIA MOLINA

Chapter Seven
Introduction

When I write
I discover, surprised,
that within me
I have an unpostponable desire
to be another woman,
a different woman,
a woman who,
who knows,
perhaps I will never be.

SILVIA MOLINA,
"THE WOMAN IN MY WRITING"

I took a taxi to Silvia Molina's house in the south of Mexico City. At the entrance to her street I had to state my business to a uniformed guard, who opened a gate to let me pass. While I searched for numbers on the impressive homes, Silvia's husband Claudio appeared in the street to guide me through their front gate, past a huge German shepherd, through another locked door, down a hall, and into a true sanctum sanctorum, isolated from noise and intruders. It was a comfortable study, with two easy chairs and rows and rows of books. The desk was covered with neat stacks of papers, a computer, and a printer. Silvia appeared soon, and after the introductions, we sat facing each other, with the tape recorder between us. That machine and something else—a reserve that floated in the air—were in the way and I couldn't get past the barrier.

Silvia is a slender woman, of medium height, wavy brown hair, and pleasant eyes hidden behind huge glasses. She wore jeans, a beautifully embroidered sweater, and a bulky winter jacket. She was sleepy, having just risen from her nap, and she was having trouble getting warm in spite of the balmy weather so typical of her native city.

Silvia's parents had come from opposite ends of the country to meet and marry in Mexico City, where Silvia was born in October of 1946. Her mother's family—including three generals from the Mexican Revolution—was from Sonora, in northern Mexico. Silvia has researched and written about her mother's side of the family in her 1987 novel *La familia vino del norte* (the family came from the north). From the other extreme of Mexico came her father's family. Her father, Héctor Pérez Martínez, was governor of the state of Campeche from 1939 to 1943, and he became secretary of the interior in President Miguel Alemán's cabinet in 1946. He died of cardiac arrest in 1948, when Silvia was only one year and a few months old. Silvia's search for her father's true, un-whitewashed identity is chronicled in her novel *Imagen de Héctor* (image of Hector, 1990).

Although she initiated her education in anthropology, Silvia received her degree in Hispanic language and literature from the National Autonomous University of Mexico (the UNAM). She won a national literary prize, the Xavier Villaurrutia, for her first novel, *La mañana debe seguir gris* (1977), translated with the title *Gray Skies Tomorrow*. It is a fictionalized account of her tragic relationship with the Mexican poet José Carlos Becerra, who died in a car accident. Her novel *Ascensión Tun* (1981) (the title is an indigenous boy's name) is about the caste wars between the Mayans and the *mestizos* in the Yucatán Peninsula in the nineteenth century. Various points of view are presented by different narrators, and a modern-day historian pulls all the pieces together.

Silvia also has written short stories, essays, and children's literature, and she participated in a creative experiment, a 1988 collective novel called *El hombre equivocado* (the mistaken man). Silvia has been awarded writing fellowships by the Mexican Center for Writers in Mexico City (1979–80) and the International Writing Program at the University of Iowa (1990). She has been a visiting professor at Brigham Young University in Utah, and she has taught creative writing and pre-Columbian literature at the UNAM from 1979 to the present. She is also the director of the publishing house Ediciones Corunda.

Silvia has gained the attention and respect of literary critics in the United States as well as in Mexico. With the exception of one extremely negative review,[1] literary scholars have been impressed by her narrative talents. Vicente Francisco Torres, who included a chapter about Silvia's work in his book on Mexican narrative, has praised *La familia vino del norte* for its "revealing account of Dorotea's contradictions; its unpretentious tone, so unadorned that it sometimes reads like a love story; and her expert manipulation of the ambiguity of the family" (1991, 154).[2]

---

[1] *I am referring to Christopher Domínguez Michale's article "Silvia Molina y la nueva retórica femenina,"* Proceso 27 (July 1987): 58–59.
[2] *This is my translation, as are all others in this part, unless otherwise noted.*

INTRODUCTION

John S. Brushwood included a discussion of *Ascensión Tun* in his book about Mexican novels, *La novela mexicana (1967–1982)*, and Reinhard Teichmann of UCSB has published an article about Silvia's work and an interview with her. Silvia's novels have been used in literature classes at several universities in Mexico, including the UNAM. A movie director offered to make a film of *Gray Skies Tomorrow,* but he wanted to make so many changes in the story that Silvia decided to cancel that project.

Silvia is very efficient about managing her time, as she juggles classes, editing, writing, and raising her two daughters. As we talk, she is interrupted by her family, the telephone, and somebody at the door, but she manages to return quickly and pick up where she left off, not wasting a minute. She speaks as she writes, with simple, direct language and a serious tone. Her former teacher, Elena Poniatowska, has described Silvia and her writing in a poetic way:

> Silvia's language is like her: tranquil, without extravagant gestures, without extreme violence. Silvia, introverted and timid, modest and quiet, looks inward. Her glasses amplify her gaze, which is attentive to her surroundings; nevertheless, what she perceives is immediately assimilated and processed in an almost imperceptible way. Actually, Silvia pays close attention to that other Silvia that she is constructing within herself. Her novels are, in some way, an interior process, an excavation to expose the tin struggles, the gray skies forever, the turtles on which Ascensión Tun must have ridden. (6)[3]

Silvia is an intense woman, very focused, yet pleasant and generous. I wish I could have known her better, much better, but that would have taken a lot of time, because we are both shy. By the end of the interview, the reserve was still in place, and our friendship, like the characters she invents in her novels, was something that should have been, or could have been, if only I lived in Mexico City and both of us had less complicated days.

---

[3]*Poniatowska is referring to several of Silvia's works: a collection of short stories called* Lides de estaño *(tin struggles), an essay on turtles, and two novels already mentioned.*

SILVIA MOLINA

At the end of our interview, she called a cab for me, and escorted me out the front door, past the German shepherd, through the garden, and out the heavy metal gate. The cabdriver negotiated his way down the narrow street, past the guard and the outer gate. Then we were speeding across a sprawling, heavily polluted metropolis, obviously plagued by poverty and crime. Silvia has to make her way through this threatening labyrinth regularly in order to perform her teaching and editing duties, and yet she has created a secure sanctuary for her writing, far removed from honking horns and exhaust fumes. Virginia Woolf would say that she has achieved "a room of one's own," which, in addition to economic independence, is so essential to a woman's success as an author.

CHAPTER EIGHT

INTERVIEW
SILVIA MOLINA

SILVIA MOLINA

KG: How did you begin to write, and what was your inspiration?[1]

SM: Like the majority of writers, I began to write when I was very young, but my first serious attempt at writing was when I read José Agustín. That was the first time that I recognized myself as a participant in Mexican literature. I recognized myself in his pages and then I wrote my first novel, which I called *Esos fueron los días* (those were the days) because there was a song by that name that was very popular at the time. In that novel I told a story similar to *De perfil* (in profile).[2] It wasn't the same story, but it was similar because it was about my group of friends, how they got together and how they had all separated later. But of course I didn't know how to write and I thought José Agustín wrote like he spoke. And it was the first time that I did an intense writing exercise like that, because every afternoon I would shut myself up to write my book; and I wrote it in the form of a book, I folded the paper in half, and I wrote the page number on the bottom of each half. I put that novel away and I never imagined that I was going to be a professional writer, but that's how I really began to write.

KG: Do you recognize a particular precursor, such as José Agustín?

SM: Yes, it would be José Agustín, but not because we have the same style. I didn't use language the way the writers of the *Onda* did; they broke with the previous model and used a very innovative language, very full of neologisms, foreign words, and all that.[3] But I consider myself a sister to José Agustín in regard to themes, because my first two novels were about young people who rebelled against their families, against institutions. In that sense, I consider Agustín to be my precursor.

---

[1] *This interview took place in August 1992.*
[2] *De perfil is a novel by the Mexican author José Agustín.*
[3] *La Onda, literally "the wave," was a group of young Mexican writers who began to write in the 1960s and became known for their iconoclastic attitudes and nontraditional language, such as street slang. They include writers such as José Agustín, Gustavo Sainz, Parménides García Saldaña, and Jesús Luis Benítez.*

INTERVIEW

KG: Have you met him?

SM: Yes, I met him a long time after I wrote my first novel, which was in preparatory school. In college I studied anthropology and later I went to Europe. When I came back I got married, and some friends told me about a writing workshop with José Agustín. I registered for the workshop, but José Agustín had a fellowship in Iowa that year, so he didn't give the classes and I didn't meet him that year. I met him a long time later.

KG: Do you also have female precursors?

SM: I couldn't say that any Mexican women writers have had a marked influence on me, but I recognize Elena Garro as someone who has affected me.[4] In the first place because I met her when I was fourteen years old. I lived in Paris then, and Elena Garro lived there, and you probably know that Elena was a woman full of vitality and intelligence, and even though I was just a fourteen-year-old girl, she treated me as if I were an adult. She asked me what I wanted to drink, whisky or vodka, and she told me all her stories about her adventures with the *campesinos* (people who work in the fields) in Morelia, and all that. At the time I was very ignorant, and I didn't know that Elena Garro was a great writer. It was her personality that captivated me at first. I wanted to be like Elena Garro when I grew up. Then, a long time later when I read *Recollections of Things to Come,* that novel had very special resonance for me. First because I knew her, but also because it seemed to be the most interesting novel written by a Mexican woman. I couldn't recognize a feminine voice in the novel, and it seemed very interesting to me. I lived in the city when I was young, but I spent many weekends in the country, and I knew a little about life in the country because of my experiences. I had heard about the Cristero

---

[4]*Garro is a well-known Mexican writer, born in Puebla in 1920, who resides in Paris. Her novels include* Testimonios sobre Mariana *(testimony about Mariana),* La casa junto al río *(the house next to the river),* Reencuentro de personajes *(reencounter with characters), and a novel translated with the title* Recollections of Things to Come.

Revolt[5] and all that, and I thought it was a brilliant work by a woman; I couldn't believe it. I read the novel many times; many, many times. I can't say that she's my precursor, but she does carry a lot of weight with me; I recognize her to be a great writer, and I try to emulate her, in some way. It would be ideal to write like Elena Garro.

KG: Have other writers influenced your work?

SM: Well, I had several teachers, like Elena Poniatowska and Hugo Hiriart,[6] but somebody who has confirmed my vision of literature is Jean Rhys.[7] [When I started writing] I hadn't read her, and one problem that I have with my writing is that everybody thinks that it is autobiographical, which it is, in part, but in the majority of my writing I am playing at inventing myself as I write. It's a chance for me to live intensely some stories that life hasn't presented to me, or that were given to me in another way, and writing has allowed me to relive those things, perhaps as I would have liked to live them, you see? Then when I read Jean Rhys's first novel, I never imagined that she was inventing. It fascinated me, I liked it because she breaks with the vision of woman in literature as a docile, noble creature, influenced by her family and everything. I read all of her works, and I thought that I knew her very well, until I finally realized that she had invented herself completely, so much so that she forbade them to write her biography because she didn't want the public to see that she was different from the protagonists she had created. I was very pleased because I felt that rather than being a strange phenomenon I was somebody connected to another writer in a different country.

KG: I have read that there is a contradiction between the way

---

[5] *A series of battles fought in the late 1920s between the government and church-supported rebels over privileges of the Catholic church in Mexico, and over control of Mexican society.*

[6] *Hugo Hiriart (1942–) is a contemporary Mexican writer whose most recent works include* Vivir y beber *(living and drinking [1988]) and* Ambar *(amber [1990]).*

[7] *Jean Rhys (1894–1979) was born in the West Indies and lived much of her life in England. She is best known for her novels* After Leaving Mr. Mackenzie *(1937) and* Wide Sargasso Sea *(1966).*

INTERVIEW

Jean Rhys writes and the way she lived. In other words, like you said, she invented another life for herself, an alternative, a road that she would have liked to have taken. I see that in your work, also.

How were you affected by the massacre of 1968?

SM: It didn't really affect me much. At the time I was studying at the National School of Anthropology and History, but I really wasn't connected to the student movement. I didn't actually understand the importance of the movement until much later. My school was very involved in the protests, it shut down, and that's when I went to Europe. It wasn't until I came back that I realized the effects of the movement, because as a consequence of 1968 there was a new awareness in art and literature in Mexico, and they began literary workshops. My style was formed in a literary workshop with Elena Poniatowska and Hugo Hiriart, and that was thanks to the events of 1968. But I wasn't a participant in '68, I don't know what world I was living in then, but it wasn't really a political world.

KG: Does that event appear in any of your works?

SM: It is mentioned in *Gray Skies Tomorrow,* because the protagonist is a bourgeois girl, as I am—I am a bourgeois woman, I can't hide it—and the rupture with her family allows her to cry about her father and also to cry about her fellow students killed in '68. She becomes aware both of her family's reality and of her country's reality.

KG: Do you deviate from traditional discourse in a conscious manner? When you are writing, are you aware that what you are writing is different from traditional discourse?

SM: I'm not sure what you call traditional discourse.

KG: Masculine, patriarchal discourse, that is found in the great novels that we have to read in literature classes, all that they teach us in school. Sometimes when I write I contradict all that I have been told; it's a protest, a counter-discourse, something different. Sometimes I am conscious of that, analytically, and other times I get lost in my writing and I am not thinking about that, I am just writing.

SM: No, I am not conscious of it. I don't intend to write a counter-proposal, I am simply expressing myself. What has happened to me is that in a lot of my literature the theme of identity is essential, even though I haven't planned that. When I finish a story or novel that is very different from previous efforts, I realize that the main character is always trying to find her true identity. I think that is a product of my own biography, it's not something that I propose to do, and yet, there it is.

KG: Many writers are surprised by what the critics perceive in their works, because many times the themes are not conscious ones.

Do you consider yourself a feminist or a humanist?

SM: I don't consider myself a feminist in the traditional sense of the word, no. I don't belong to any feminist movement. Nevertheless, I recognize many things in the feminists, and I believe that many of my characters are feminists in the sense that they try to find their own values and to express themselves, on a par with men. They try to find their freedom within the society and the time period that they have to live.

KG: One thing that I have noticed in some women writers recently—such as the Chilean author Isabel Allende—is that they are becoming more "humanist" in the sense that they are including men as complete characters who support the female protagonists, and the men aren't simply the villains who impede the woman's progress. I consider that to be very healthy. They are exploring new and liberating ways of forming a couple.

SM: Yes, I believe that the solution will be the couple. I am lucky because my companion, my husband Claudio, respects my profession a lot and he has never been opposed to it; on the contrary, he has always supported me in everything.

KG: Yes, you are lucky. How do you combine your personal and professional lives? Do you have a routine for writing?

SM: When I am working on something, I usually write at night, but if I am too caught up in what I am doing, I will steal some time in the morning. I run the publishing house Ediciones Corunda and I have to go to the office; but I can't write in my office, with the phone calls and other

INTERVIEW

interruptions. So I get up early and write one or two hours, and then go to the office. Then I write again at night. My daughters are almost adults now, but for many years I wrote after I put them to bed. I can write for three, four, or five hours, I don't have a limit, and many times my husband comes down and asks me, "When are you going to sleep?" Time goes by and I don't notice, but if I am not working on something I am very irregular; I don't force myself to write every day. A week can go by and I won't sit down at the computer to write. Things accumulate, and when I finally sit down it's because I am saturated and I need to release the writing.

KG: How much of *La familia vino del norte* (the family came from the north) is based on fact?

SM: The anecdote comes from a true family story. My mother is from Sonora and she had three brothers, revolutionary generals, who left Sonora for the [Mexican] revolution [of 1910] when they were very young: twelve, thirteen, and fourteen years old. One of those three generals was a Serranista, from Francisco Serrano's group.[8] Francisco Serrano used to play marbles at my uncle's house, and they were very close friends. All the revolutionaries from Sonora knew each other quite well, and they formed a strong clan. This uncle of mine was about to die in Huitzilac[9] with Francisco Serrano, but somebody let him know that [Obregón's supporters] had prepared a trap, and he was able to escape. He went to Veracruz with some other friends and then later he returned to his mother's home, and he hid in the basement for one year.

When I was a little girl I always heard that my uncle had been shut up in the cellar for a year, but I never knew why. I started to investigate, because I thought if you hide in a basement for a year it's because you have done something bad, or something good, but for some reason you are being pursued. When I found out that he had been a Serranista, I

---

[8] In 1927 Francisco Serrano led an attempt to prevent the reelection of Alvaro Obregón. He and most of his followers were killed or exiled.

[9] The place where Serrano was executed, on the Cuernavaca–Mexico City highway in the state of Morelos, after he was apprehended in Cuernavaca.

had to investigate a lot about the Mexican Revolution because we are taught very little in school. Once I had the story of that character, my problem was to tell the story without giving a history lesson. It was hard for me to find the right tone. First I wrote the novel in third person, then in second person, and I didn't know how to tell the story until I overheard a conversation in which a girl said, "My grandfather did such-and-such," and then I realized that was the tone; the narrator could tell her grandfather's story, and other voices could enter, also. But that real story is only the point of departure, because the house that I describe does not exist, the family as I describe it does not exist, and I did not have a relationship with a newspaperman, either.

KG: Could you tell me your uncle's name?

SM: The character is actually based on all three of my uncles, but the one who hid in the cellar was Manuel Celis, and he really was a revolutionary general. For my children this is all history, but I actually knew many revolutionary generals. My real name is Silvia Pérez Celis; Pérez, from my father, and Celis, from my mother; so he was my mother's brother. My real last name is Pérez, but I never use it.

KG: So you prefer Molina?

SM: Yes, it's my husband's last name, and Silvia Molina is like my pen name.

KG: Are the family photos authentic in *La familia vino del norte*?

SM: Yes, the photos are authentic, and it is a game. I used photographs both in *La familia vino del norte* and *Imagen de Héctor* (image of Hector), and they are relatives of mine, those are my real grandparents. The one with the grandfather's name was actually his brother, but they were all my relatives. And in the second part, the photos of real generals like Serrano are authentic. I wanted to play a game, in order to make the story more credible, and that's why I also put a chronology at the end of *Ascención Tun*,[10] it was a list of names, and I gave

---

[10] *Ascención Tun was the name of an indigenous boy in the novel. Ascensión is Spanish for "ascension," and* tun *means "rock" in the Mayan language, like the English name Peter.*

INTERVIEW

biographies to the fictional characters, as if they had really existed. And the photographs in the other novels were a game to make the story more true to life.

KG: Can you tell me more about the process of combining history with fiction?

SM: Perhaps because of my anthropological studies, history has always interested me as a framework for another story. When I wrote *Gray Skies Tomorrow*, I realized that everybody who reads in Mexico would already know that José Carlos Becerra was a real person who died in an automobile accident in Italy, so everybody would know how the story ended.[11] I wanted to overtake that process and tell the whole story at the beginning, but in the simplest way possible so that the reader would know the story but read it again afterwards. In addition, I used news releases from Mexico, Australia, and from all over the world in order to create a historical framework for the novel, to situate it in a time period. There are certain historical truths that one cannot falsify. You can invent many things, but you can't say, for example, that [President Venustiano] Carranza did something that he didn't do in real life, because then your novel will be a failure. Therefore, one can't really alter historical truth, but it can serve as a background to give more intensity to another story.

One of my intentions when I wrote *La familia vino del norte* was to show that Mexican writers—both men and women—of my generation grew up with an official story, taught to us at school, and everything that wasn't in that official story was taboo, it was forbidden. The story of Serrano as told at this time is completely different from what we learned in school. We learned that Serrano was a traitor and now it turns out that Serrano was practically a hero; he opposed Obregón's reelection because he and the grandfather in my story and all the others went out to fight the revolution in order to oppose the reelection of

---

[11]*José Carlos Becerra (1937–70), born in Tabasco, Mexico, was in Europe in 1970 on a Guggenheim fellowship to finish his collection of poems,* El otoño recorre las islas *(autumn tours the islands), which was published posthumously. Prior to that trip, he had published* Relación de los hechos *(statement of the facts).*

[Porfirio] Díaz. They all fought for an ideal which their own leader wanted to betray. So my intention was to tell the other part of the story, that part which is not told, to break the taboo of the official story and to tell what is not told in the history books. Some of those generals were completely anonymous, but that heritage is still ours.

KG: Is it true that Manuel Celis is not mentioned in the history books?

SM: No, he is not mentioned.

KG: In *Gray Skies Tomorrow,* is the protagonist based on reality?

SM: Yes.

KG: But you don't mention her name?

SM: No, the story is based on my own experiences. I lived in England at that time, I knew José Carlos Becerra, but what happens in the novel is not what happened in real life. Even though I used some names from real life, which is a departure from traditional Mexican literature, I didn't use my name because I made up the story, I told it the way I would have liked to have lived it.

KG: So you don't want people to think that you really lived that story . . .

SM: Well, it's an autobiographical novel, I can't deny that, but just because it uses real life as a point of departure doesn't mean that it is all true. In that case I would have written a chronicle, or something like that, but in this novel I am a fictional character, an invention, like Jean Rhys's characters. It's incredible, isn't it?

KG: Yes, I understand. The narrator of *La familia vino del norte* admits that the fox, the god of cunning and treachery, is also her god. Would you say that the fox is also your god?

SM: I believe so. I think that it is really the god of all writers, that's why I used that quote. Because a writer has an obligation to tell the story without qualms. For example, when I wrote *Gray Skies Tomorrow* I was married, and so I could have held back the story out of consideration for my husband. How could I publish a story that is part of my real life? But I believe that my obligation as a writer is to be faithful to the writing. *La familia vino del norte* was also a story that was taboo in my

INTERVIEW

family. They had a reason for not talking about it, because Serrano was condemned. To speak of Serrano was to speak of a traitor. My family never told the truth, that's why we didn't know it, even though it was really an honorable story, all of them are heroes now.

I took the quote about the fox from a story by Boris Pilnyak.[12] It is about a Japanese writer who is very successful because of a story that he wrote about his Russian wife. When she finds out what he wrote, his wife leaves him and goes back to Russia; but he wrote what he had to write, don't you think so? But yes, I believe that the fox is my god in some ways because I have never written my own truth. As I was trying to write my autobiography in *SM: De cuerpo entero* (SM: in full view),[13] I thought, am I really capable of writing my own truth? Who knows? Truth is hard. It's really easy to transform reality. I don't have a lot of imagination, I don't know how to make up stories out of nothing. To adapt or appropriate a reality and to make it mine, thanks to literature, that I have learned. And I feel that when I adapt these stories from reality, my first obligation is to tell what I have to tell. If I am going to affect one of my daughters, or my mother, or my husband, well, I hope they will forgive me some day, if they can, but it's difficult.

KG: My interpretation of your work is that you imply, "Everybody is lying, and I am lying, too." You admit that you are offering just one more version of reality, and it's not the definitive view. The reader has to weave your version together with another version, and another and another, in order to fabricate his or her own reality and to participate in the creation of meaning.

SM: Yes, that's true.

KG: Dorotea, the narrator of *La familia vino del norte*, has to

---

[12] *Boris Pilnyak was a pseudonym for Boris Andreevich Vogau (1894–1937), a Russian author whose translated works include* Tales of the Wilderness, The Naked Year, *and* The Volga Flows into the Caspian Sea.

[13] *Ediciones Corunda is publishing a series of autobiographies by Mexican writers. Each writer is identified in the title by his/her initials, followed by the words* De cuerpo entero.

read foreign literature, such as Jean Rhys's *After Leaving Mr. Mackenzie,* in order to find a positive role model. Have you noticed the lack of positive female role models in Mexican literature?

SM: Yes, I've noticed that a lot; for example, Isabel, the protagonist of Elena Garro's *Recollections of Things to Come,* is converted into stone; she pays for her sin, and her sin was desiring freedom. And there is another interesting character, Elena Poniatowska's Jesusa Palancares, but there's no model—I don't know if it's horrible to say this—for a woman of my class, for all of us women writers who have developed in the bourgeois medium. There is no model that is appropriate for our social environment. That's one reason why I am so impressed with Jean Rhys, although she is very harsh. She tells the truth, her true sentiments about alcoholism, about her mean spirit, about loneliness which becomes surrender to any man. As she passes from hotel room to hotel room in her novels, she passes from one man to another. And in spite of all that, she survives. And she expresses it openly; that is completely forbidden for Mexican women, because of the way we are raised. Through her, I discovered a different model of woman, because I am all of that also, we are all equal in our feelings. I believe that women's emotions are universal, even though few admit their true intimate feelings; sometimes we are terrible. I am pleased that Jean Rhys reveals a woman who could be me, although I don't dare to show it and even in my own writing I don't dare to express it very much, but she made me recognize myself.

KG: I was pleased to find Dorotea in your novel because I was looking for a positive model. In so many books there are women who are beaten, abandoned, prostituted, or lost to alcoholism or insanity, but there are no women who forge ahead, who shape their own future, who are active and can take control of their own existence. Dorotea is a breath of fresh air. But it's a little ironic that your protagonist had to resort to reading literature from other countries in order to find a model, and she is actually a more positive model than Jean Rhys's protagonists. Do you plan to write more stories or novels with positive role models for women?

INTERVIEW

SM: I have just given a collection of short stories to the publishing house Cal y Arena, called *Un hombre cerca* (a man nearby) [released in fall 1992].
KG: Is that the title of one of the stories?
SM: No, but they are all stories in which there is a man nearby, and some of them have positive female characters, but I think that they are also about problems of a couple. For example, one is about a woman who has an affair, and another is about a man who has an affair. Some of them are about other relatives, like a father or an uncle.
KG: Do some of those men support the women?
SM: Yes, although it's not a couple situation, but in one case an uncle supports his niece, and he is a very beloved character for me.
KG: Do you plan to write another novel?
SM: I am writing a novel, but I have it on the back burner right now. It is about a woman who receives a letter from a man who gives a pseudonym and a post office box number, and he asks her to answer certain questions about her life. She answers him and says that she will go along with his game, but he has to answer the same questions that he asks her, and both of them may tell the truth or not, as they wish. We never see his letters, but she refers to them in her letters [and the reader can infer the contents]. At the end of the story it turns out that it's the woman's [estranged] husband who is writing to her. But I've abandoned the novel for a while, because I'm trying to finish my autobiographical essay.
KG: Going back to the idea of positive role models, in your opinion, why does Dorotea manage to escape the oppressive environment in which she finds herself?
SM: Because I am always struggling to get out of there, I mean, I think the death of her grandfather is a turning point in Dorotea's awareness. For me, the grandfather's death is a metaphor for the death of the revolution. My whole generation grew up with the messages, "We are all the Revolution, The Revolution isn't over, The achievements of the Revolution continue"; they were slogans being driven into us constantly in Mexico. However, what I felt was that the

revolution was being held up by clothespins, so much so that they have just changed the Constitution in regard to the land reform, which was one of the principal ideas of the Mexican Revolution. So I wanted to symbolize the death throes of the revolution with the moribund state of the grandfather, who is maintained with intravenous feeding, oxygen, and blood transfusions; he is dying but everybody wants to keep him alive, like the Mexican Revolution. When he dies, Dorotea becomes aware of the family oppression. She realizes that those family members who have gathered around the grandfather don't feel love or loyalty to him, they are just trying to get something from him. When he dies, Dorotea also realizes that her grandfather failed, too, because he betrayed the ideals for which he fought in the revolution.

    She realizes, then, that she is a product of all that, and she has to accept herself as she is. I believe that what gives Dorotea the strength to free herself from her family and from [her lover] Manuel, and to tell the real story, is knowing who she is. She is a product of an inheritance which she did nothing to obtain, and at the same time she is authentic, in the sense of doing what she wishes, not what society plans for her. She finally accepts her grandparents' money, but she uses it to further her career as a historian, she doesn't betray her goals. Perhaps the model that you and I can follow is not that of our mothers, nor of our grandmothers; we don't have a nearby point of reference that we can follow. And we don't want to give our daughters an out-of-date model, either.

KG: Is it true that your family didn't support your professional aspirations?

SM: They never were opposed, but they never supported me, either. Like many women, I wasn't raised to be a professional, but rather to get married. In spite of the fact that my father was a writer, my family never thought of the possibility that I might be a writer, even when I began to write. They think I'm strange, to this date I am somebody different from them. They didn't put up roadblocks, but they didn't encourage me, either.

KG: Were there any obstacles in your path to becoming a writer?

INTERVIEW

SM: I have had a lot of luck. My husband has always supported me in everything, and it was easy for me to publish *Gray Skies Tomorrow;* the publishers liked it immediately because it was about real people. For a long time I wrote alone, my generation always worked alone, not supported by other writers, not knowing that there were others producing at the same time. But there were no real obstacles. Of course it would be ideal to be able to write full time, but that seems impossible in Mexico; most of us are editors, professors, or bureaucrats, and it's utopia to be able to dedicate yourself only to writing. But I've received the Villaurrutia Prize, the fellowship in Iowa, I went to teach in Utah with the Mormons; so I feel that I am lucky, I can't complain.

KG: Is your book *Imagen de Héctor* (image of Hector) autobiographical?

SM: It is autobiographical, but there is fiction in the book, also. I didn't know my father and he was always a myth for me. That always hindered me when I was a girl, that's why I changed my name to Silvia Molina, because it bothered me that everybody said, "Ah, you're Hector's daughter." I was always Hector's daughter, never Silvia. I believe that's a problem for us, the children of men who are well known in politics or in intellectual circles. The figure of the father weighs on us a lot.

I always thought that in order to be a politician you needed to be rough—politics is a very difficult road—and it seemed impossible to me that my father could have been as marvelous as they said he was, and still be a politician. And so the search for my father's true identity was a way of settling an account in my autobiography, to find out who he really was. My brothers and sister had an image of my father which was very different from the one that I discovered in my search, because I read all of his books and I talked with other writers who had known him and I looked in the library for all the information about his governorship in Campeche. Everything about my father in the novel is totally true, but one character who is mainly fictitious is Miss Heidi. I did have a nanny when I was born, and she was German like Miss Heidi, but the strong

relationship between the nanny and the young girl is my invention. It was an element that I needed in order to bring out the character of the young girl a little, but I never really saw Miss Heidi again, nor did she come back to get me.
KG: With which of your protagonists do you identify the most?
SM: I think I identify the most with Dorotea, my heroine.
KG: Like several other authors—Elena Garro, Rosario Castellanos, Elena Poniatowska, for example—you have identified a connection between women and other marginalized groups, like the indigenous people, and poor people. I am referring especially to *Ascensión Tun*. Do you think that this recognition is mutual?
SM: No, I don't think so, because within their group women are still marginalized.
KG: That's too bad, because we women often identify with minorities, but they don't seem to recognize the connections between us, and as you said, within their groups women are marginalized, they are treated as inferiors.

What do these groups have in common, and how can we help each other?
SM: I believe that as long as the indigenous groups don't recognize the value of their own culture, and it is not recognized by others, they will continue to be an unappreciated minority. And it's the same for women: as long as they don't recognize the value of their work, both at home and in their profession, they will continue to be undervalued. There are a lot of different aspects to our lives, and it would help us to not denigrate any of them.
KG: What can women contribute to literature? How is their writing different?
SM: I feel that women's contribution is sharing the interior reality of women. There are men who have written marvelous works about women, but I believe that women writers can reveal how women really are, and how they function when they have a man nearby—like in my collection of short stories—and how they function with their children and what their intimate world is like. I think that is an important contribution made by women writers.

INTERVIEW

Now, how is their writing different? I think that in some cases, like in mine, although my writing isn't exactly feminist, it is a little feminine, or subtle. My writing is a little delicate. I always try to take care with the writing in that sense, with the expression; sometimes I use bad words, but in general the tone of my voice in writing is delicate, and perhaps my point of view is that of a woman, which is not bad because we have lived for centuries with men's point of view and the masculine tone. Referring back to Jean Rhys, what reading other women's work has done for me is to help me know myself better.
KG: A lot of women's literature is not appreciated by some men; they don't identify with the woman's experience and they feel that the book is not speaking to them. But I believe that men can become familiarized with the female experience and thus they can learn to appreciate literature written by women.

What advice would you give a woman writer who is just starting her career?
SM: I would tell her to read a lot, that's very important, and then I would say that she should be critical with herself, but not so much that it blocks her writing. She shouldn't try to write a masterpiece the first time.

CHAPTER NINE

HISTORY AND HERSTORY: SILVIA MOLINA'S *LA FAMILIA VINO DEL NORTE* AND *IMAGEN DE HÉCTOR*

It is the project of
twentieth-century women writers
to solve the contradiction
between love and quest
and to replace
the alternate endings
in marriage or death
that are their cultural legacy
from nineteenth-century
life and letters by offering
a different set of choices.
They invent a complex
of narrative acts
with psychosocial meanings,
which will be studied here
as "writing beyond the ending."

RACHEL BLAU DUPLESSIS,
WRITING BEYOND THE ENDING

LA FAMILIA VINO DEL NORTE

LA FAMILIA VINO DEL NORTE (THE FAMILY CAME FROM THE NORTH) is a complex novel within a novel with several different layers of fiction that interact with other texts, historical as well as fictional. The protagonist, Dorotea Leyva, has embarked upon a search for her grandfather's personal and political secret: Why did General Teodoro Leyva spend a year hiding in his mother's basement? With the help and hindrance of her lover, the news writer and publisher called Manuel, Dorotea's project broadens to include a search for her personal identity, which results in her own declaration of independence. In order to break the bonds that hold her down, Dorotea must struggle against her family's and Manuel's efforts to control her, while unraveling an intricate tapestry of lies, official stories and silence, and overcoming a series of betrayals that began long before she was born.

In reaction to an article that Manuel wrote about her grandfather, Dorotea decides to publish a description of her own personal and historical search, and she gives her narration the same title as Molina's novel, "La familia vino del norte." Dorotea's text—an exercise in alternative discourse, because it opposes Manuel's article—is embedded in Molina's novel, and framed by letters to and from Manuel. Within the framework of the novel, Dorotea's discourse is presented as nonfiction, although we learn later in the text that Dorotea has taken some liberties with her narrative, and Manuel has exercised some censorship, including having his name changed.

Molina's novel, then, consists of an epigraph (a quote by Boris Pilnyak), a prologue (letters to and from Manuel), Dorotea's text, and an epilogue (a final letter from Dorotea to Manuel). Dorotea's text includes two pages of photographs and her narrative is divided into twenty-six sections. Section 25 includes quotes from two texts exterior to Dorotea's narrative but within Silvia Molina's fictional space; they are the diary of Teodoro Leyva and the article by Manuel. There are also some passages that have been omitted from Dorotea's narrative, on Manuel's request, which tell the story of Manuel's rise to power in the newspaper world.

By means of this complex process of imbedding texts within her narrative and referring to other texts that have been suppressed, Molina has created an alternative narrative structure that could be defined as follows:

> A structure that in important ways is not modeled on masculine sexuality (as is the "classic" linear and teleological plot, with its situation, rising action, climax, and denouement) and that resists the [dominant] ideologies encoded in the "classic" structure by refusing to make a univocal revelation the point of the whole story, in this way refusing to privilege a single version of "the truth" as definitive.
> (Hite 165)[1]

The traditional, stable point of view is subverted by this alternative structure, by means of which Molina emphasizes the concept that the truth is not a fixed reality. The author thus questions the hegemony of history and the claim of some historians that they convey definitive truth. "Art gives voice to what history has denied, silenced or persecuted. Art rescues truth from the clutches of history's lies," according to Carlos Fuentes (82), and Molina uses literature to demonstrate that idea.

Molina also is presenting ideological alternatives, as she creates a protagonist who rejects the traditional choices open to women, a process that has been called "writing beyond the ending":

> Writing beyond the ending means the transgressive invention of narrative strategies, strategies that express critical dissent from dominant narrative. These tactics, among them reparenting, woman-to-woman and brother-to-sister bonds, and forms of the communal protagonist, take issue

---

[1] *Hite refers to "masculinist" ideologies where I have inserted "dominant." I prefer the latter term because there are also male writers who have created alternative narrative structures. Carlos Fuentes and Julio Cortázar are two obvious examples.*

with the mainstays of the social and ideological organization of gender, as these appear in fiction. (DuPlessis 5)

Molina's principal transgressive strategy is reparenting, as Dorotea's investigation leads her to discover gaps in her own childhood, and she attempts to fill those voids herself. There is also an interesting parental relationship between the author and her protagonist, because Dorotea's grandfather is based on Molina's uncle, which places Dorotea one generation beyond Molina. Thus, the writer has created her own literary daughter, and in the process, she has reparented herself, creating a character she would like to be.

Within Dorotea's narrative there are many bifurcations. Teodoro Leyva comes from the north with two families, his relatives and his military/political allies. His official story has been obfuscated by lies and silence. Although his name does not appear in the history books, the story of the Serranista revolt of 1927 is featured in many works about Alvaro Obregón and the Mexican Revolution. Because he participated in this revolt, General Leyva was forced into hiding for a year. In his article, Manuel attempts to supplement the official story by revealing the human side of the story, that is, the personal experience of General Leyva during and after the revolt. Dorotea then uses Manuel's article and her grandfather's diary to piece together what she calls the "real story." She chops Manuel's article up into little pieces, and uses the excerpts that are useful to her. In contrast, she organizes and expands her grandfather's diary, creating a more cohesive narrative:

> I know that I have literally shredded Manuel's essay, and not for revenge, but for convenience. . . . While I made mincemeat out of him, I gave everything I had to my grandfather, in order to carefully reconstruct the fragments of his diary. (146)[2]

---

[2]*Page numbers in this section, if not otherwise identified, are from* La familia vino del norte, *2nd ed. (Mexico City: Aguilar, León y Cal, 1989). All translations are mine, if not otherwise noted. Due to the length of this manuscript, I have not included the original Spanish unless there is not a clear translation in English. The reader may refer to the novel, using the page numbers provided.*

At one point, she even corrects a crucial assertion in her grandfather's diary. Teodoro Leyva wrote that he did not support the Serranista revolt. Dorotea had proof that he did support the revolt, and upon reading his words, she comments wryly, "I only would have believed that when I was a very little girl, or I would have accepted it about any man other than my grandfather" (141). She later concludes that everything else that General Leyva wrote was true (144), and she corroborates this with information obtained from her relatives and from the family maid. Thus, she transforms both Manuel's and her grandfather's texts, generating in the process her own alternative discourse.

Dorotea's narrative also bifurcates as she describes how she and Manuel embark upon not only a historical investigation but also a modern-day romance. Both the investigation and the love affair lead Dorotea toward her own self-affirmation and her eventual independence; thus she manages to "write beyond the ending," creating new choices for herself.

Besides the intricate relationships between the different texts within Molina's novel, there is also an intertextual relationship between her narrative and that of several exterior texts. Molina quotes the twentieth-century Russian author Boris Pilnyak in the epigraph: "The fox is the god of cunning and betrayal: if the spirit of the fox penetrates a man, that man's race is condemned. The fox is the god of writers!" (n.p.)

Dorotea reveals who the fox is in her first letter to Manuel: "It all began when I realized that the fox, the god of cunning and betrayal, was your god" (13). She insists on this comparison when she refers to beginning to work for Manuel: "It was then that the god of cunning and betrayal, without my realizing it, came into my life" (23).

Later Dorotea buys the book *Caoba* (mahogany), by Boris Pilnyak, and she mentions one of the stories to Manuel, revealing her interest in writing. Manuel makes fun of her, and expresses his own belief that a writer must be willing to put writing ahead of everything else, foreshadowing his betrayal of Dorotea.

The epigraph to Molina's novel is the final paragraph of Pilnyak's story, whose title in English is "A Story About How Stories Come

HISTORY AND HERSTORY

To Be Written."³ This tale, which is metafiction just like Molina's text, describes how a Japanese man writes a novel based on his Russian wife's life, including intimate details, but without her permission. When she finds out about the deceit, she leaves him and returns to her native Russia.

In Molina's text, Manuel betrays Dorotea in a similar way, by publishing his article about Teodoro Leyva, using information they had obtained together, but without giving her any credit. Dorotea refers to fairy tales, Greek tragedies, and Boris Pilnyak in order to explain Manuel's treachery:

> My relationship with Manuel became so extreme that it was hell. Thus, our ending wasn't like in the fairy tales, but more like the resolution in Greek tragedy, except for one thing: destiny had nothing to do with our story. And like in the tale by Boris Pilnyak, Manuel did nothing more than write a "beautiful story" (of course, at the expense of ours, the personal, intimate story!). Why? Because Manuel's only god is the fox, of course. (153)

A fairy tale without a happy ending, a Greek tragedy without the force of destiny, Boris Pilnyak's "most beautiful story" at the expense of an intimate relationship; all of these intertextual references help Dorotea to understand Manuel's deceit and to generate her own side of the story:

> Since Manuel hadn't told more than one part of the story, it seemed to me, then, that I should tell the rest.
>
> For much of my life, I was caught inside a series of structures that didn't allow me to move. Now I know from experience that just the desire for change is enough to make those structures begin to break. Even though my training has taught me to proceed with rigorous objectivity in order to interpret historical facts, as I wrote this version of what Manuel

---

³This story, translated into English, can be found in Pilnyak's book *The Tale of the Unextinguished Moon and Other Stories* (New York: Washington Square, 1967), although Molina's character finds the story in Spanish, in a book called *Caoba* (mahogany).

SILVIA MOLINA

suppressed, I have re-created "my story" with luxurious freedom; therefore I don't pretend to do otherwise. Why not pay homage to the fox myself? Why shouldn't I? (153)

The reader witnesses, in this passage, Dorotea's coming into her own in several ways. She has learned to break with the traditions that limit her, she has trained herself as a historian, and she is capable of creating her own story, paying homage herself to the god of deceit. The admission that she is playing the fox's game, of course, puts into question everything else that Dorotea says, revealing her to be a creative but unreliable narrator. Since no single version of the truth is definitive, the reader is left to piece together his or her own narrative in imitation of the author's craft and the process undertaken by the narrator.

But we have more here than just several versions of fiction; Molina also presents a historical background based on verifiable facts. Francisco Serrano actually did lead a revolt in 1927 after Obregón announced his candidacy for president, defying the principle of no reelection. The revolt was swiftly squelched, and the leaders were executed or exiled. Molina uses the general outline of the revolt as a backdrop for her novel, besides including some personal details, such as the friendship between the journalist Vito Alessio Robles's daughter and President Calles's daughters. Molina also accurately portrays several historical figures—Alvaro Obregón, Plutarco Elías Calles, and General Benjamín Hill—and has them interact with her fictional characters. Molina's narrator reads several accounts of that period of history: the nonfiction work *Yesterday in Mexico*, by John W. F. Dulles; the historical novel *La sombra del caudillo* (the shadow of the leader), by Martín Luis Guzmán; and the historical play *Los relámpagos de agosto* (August lightning), by Jorge Ibargüengoitia. Although Dorotea finds no mention of her grandfather in these books, they help her understand the events leading up to Teodoro's confinement.

As Dorotea searches through family memories, she evokes an interesting interfacing of human and political history:

When I saw [my grandmother] there, suffering so much . . . I thought again about how daring and strong human beings

HISTORY AND HERSTORY

slowly burn out until they are withered like my grandmother, that woman who long ago knelt before General Calles to beg for the life of General Leyva.

When I think about that scene which was just about to change history, I realize even more how fragile and subject to daily details it is—history, of course. (122)

As Dorotea discovers the interaction between individual and collective history, she approaches a deeper understanding of human evolution and the meaning of history. After visiting her great-grandmother's house, she exclaims: "I thought that was precisely life, history: the reconstruction of ruins, an eternal new beginning of building, getting up, transforming until you discover something different" (111).

This same transformational process takes place in Molina's text. Dorotea is reconstructing her history, pulling together bits and pieces of information, discarding some, reorganizing others, finally managing to transform these disparate parts into a coherent whole, which helps to form her own identity. She is aided in her search by the inspiration found in another exterior text, a book by Jean Rhys, whose protagonist provides a positive role model:

> I went out into the garden and threw myself beneath the shade of the jacaranda tree to read Jean Rhys' novel: *After Leaving Mr. Mackenzie*. I had started reading her novels after one of Manuel's friends mentioned her to me. I saw in Ms. Rhys a model of an authentic woman. It seemed that she had lived one hundred years ahead of us Mexican women. Her worries, her problems, had nothing to do with our domestic life, with the family, with the couple as we know it. She spoke about herself without pity, without qualms. (81)

By presenting Dorotea's quest for independence, Molina provides one of the very few positive role models for women in Mexican literature. Ironically, Molina's own protagonist resorts to reading literature by foreign women such as Jean Rhys, and these books help her to analyze her own situation and to place herself in a universal context.

Dorotea's search for identity begins with the realization that her family's traditional life was a trap. Her grandfather was a patriarch, ruling over the women of the family with an iron hand. Dorotea's workaholic father and alcoholic mother tried to impose their expectations on her. The vision of her family as mummified corpses comes to the narrator in a dream.

Dorotea feels uncomfortable and out of place with her family. She remembers her grandmother always deferring to the patriarch, the other women never expressing their opinions. She asks Manuel, "Why do you suppose they teach women to deny themselves, why do they accept such denial?" (33). In spite of the anguish and uncertainty, the narrator also interprets the situation with humor:

> When I announced at home that I was going to work in a journalist's apartment (*departamento* in Spanish, which could be either apartment or department), my father raised the roof with his shouts. Naturally I sensed that I would like that job, just because my family thought it was indecent. I ended up saying that in case they didn't know, I would be working in the "Editorial Department;" and I asked myself what I was doing living at home like Daddy's little girl.
>
> For a long time I had known that it was good for me to go against the family current because everything that they despised turned out to be pleasant. (27)

The narrator's grandmother tries to coerce her back into the fold by offering her the family jewels, which Dorotea staunchly refuses because they represent the tradition that she wants to escape. Her grandmother doesn't let her off easily, however, for when she dies, her last will and testament reveals Dorotea to be her only heir. The narrator literally has a nervous breakdown, faced with this imposition of family wealth. Dorotea comments wryly: "Suddenly she had bestowed upon me with her magic wand the gift that I most scorned: material wealth" (129).

Dorotea's attempts to escape the patterns established by her family correspond closely with her efforts to create an alternative discourse, the concrete evidence of which is her manuscript called "La familia vino del norte." In fact, familial relations themselves can be interpreted as a kind of text, as Hodge and Kress have pointed out in their recent work Social Semiotics,[4] which links sociology with linguistics and literary analysis:

> But it is important to insist that the family as a set of meanings is itself a kind of text, or more precisely, an overlapping set of texts which we will term *familial texts*. . . . The familial text that children first construct is deeply learnt, and it provides the starting point for a chain of transformations that make sense of every other major social relationship. (206)

Modifications to the text can be made by any family member, according to Hodge and Kress, and generation and gender are not restricting factors, as they explain: "It is more a matter of the scope for resistance that individuals can exercise, the degree to which they can produce oppositional familial texts" (226).

Dorotea is hindered in her production of an oppositional familial text, however, by her choice of lovers. Both Manuel and her previous boyfriend try to manipulate her, to remake her into the woman they want. Dorotea's relationship with each of them is an extension of her familial text, which she can only rewrite by extricating herself. Manuel treats her like a child, trying to control what she reads, what music she buys, and what she does with her spare time. Manuel also isolates her from his newspaper world, just as her father left her out of his business.

Dorotea is also hindered by the lies and silence that are her family's means of dealing with unpleasant situations and of manipulating the children's behavior by presenting "perfect" models. The history books are also strangely silent about her grandfather's role in the revolution and its aftermath. Another significant obstacle to Dorotea's self-discovery is betrayal. Long before she was born, a complicated chain of betrayals was initiated. By declaring his intention to become president again, Alvaro Obregón betrayed the revolutionary ideal of no reelection. Several groups of anti-reelectionists, led by Francisco Serrano and

---

[4]*In* Social Semiotics, *the authors analyze many different kinds of messages, including paintings, cartoons, billboards, literary texts, and social interactions. The quotes that I have chosen are excerpts from their analysis of familial interaction in real life, but they obviously can be applied to familial interaction in literature.*

supported by Teodoro Leyva, planned to overthrow the government to prevent Obregón from taking office, which constituted both treason and betrayal of close friends. The anti-reelectionists were betrayed by a whistle-blower, and subsequently killed or exiled. Teodoro Leyva, having betrayed his old ally Obregón, remained true to his revolutionary ideals for some time but finally succumbed to political, economic, and familial pressures to become what he had detested in his youth: a rich, conservative man of leisure caught up in the political machine and married to the spoiled daughter of an hacendado (a wealthy landowner). Teodoro's son (Dorotea's father) follows in his footsteps, marrying a woman like his mother: educated in Europe and born of hacendados who once supported the dictatorship of Porfirio Díaz.

Dorotea seems to be the only one in her family who is aware of these multiple betrayals and contradictions. She turns to Manuel to help her sort them out, but he in turn betrays her both by having an affair with another woman and by publishing his infamous article.

Thus Dorotea is essentially alone in her search for understanding. She gets tidbits of information from Manuel, her grandparents before their death, her father, and the family maid, but her journey can only be completed in solitude. The narrator compares her search to taking a long trip, during which she would learn to understand life in another way, and she is aware of the connection between her investigation of her grandfather's past and her own quest for identity:

> Knowing why my grandfather was hidden, why in our family they keep secrets or they lie, why at the end of his life Teodoro Leyva turned out to be what he went forth to combat in 1910, leads me, inevitably, to the question of who I am, since I form part of that reality. (151)

Dorotea resists Manuel's attempts to control her, including the suggestion in his letter that she change her name in her manuscript. The narrator's name is important to her, as it reveals her identification with her grandfather:

HISTORY AND HERSTORY

> Actually, the two names, *Teodoro* and *Dorotea,* are nothing
> more than a play on words:
> (doro-tea-doro-teo-doro),
> full of recollections, of memories.
> Teo (that was he) - doro (I). (51–52)

The narrator's relationship with her grandfather is so close that part of her own narrative is told from his point of view. Half of section 4 and all of section 10 is narrated in the third person from Teodoro Leyva's point of view. Section 7 is narrated in the first person by Teodoro Leyva, as he told his story to Dorotea. Also, the starting point of Dorotea's narrative is her grandfather's funeral: he took his secret with him to his grave, a fact which both frustrates Dorotea and inspires her to begin her own investigation.

When he was alive, however, Teodoro had urged Dorotea to marry and give him a grandson named Teodoro. His idea of educating her was to offer her piano lessons, so she could play like her grandmother. Even though he recognized her as special, he was still encouraging her to follow the family traditions, and to live the limited life that her mother, grandmother, aunts, and female cousins were all enduring. Therefore, Dorotea had to qualify her identification with her grandfather. She needed to connect with his youth, when he stood steadfastly by his ideals, and not to be swayed by what he became in his old age. She also needed to be what her grandfather was, not what he wanted for her. Dorotea recognizes that even her grandfather had hoped for a traditional life for her: "I had to struggle for myself, in order to get out of that trap that my whole family, including my grandfather, had prepared for me" (85).

Dorotea's biggest challenge is when she becomes her grandmother's universal heir. After overcoming her crisis, she manages to use the money to further her own independence and professional aspirations. Besides buying her own condo and a car, she stops giving biology classes and dedicates her time to the study of history, her recently chosen field. She becomes a research assistant in the Institute of Historical Investigations, working on a Nahuatl project. She decides to learn Nahuatl and to specialize in the pre-Columbian period. The Nahuatl people, like the family in the novel's title, also came from the north, although long before Columbus arrived in America. The indigenous people become an alternative family for Dorotea, at least intellectually.

Manuel's alcoholism and jealousy finally result in a separation, which Dorotea reinforces by going to Paris to work with documents in Nahuatl. It is in Paris that she writes her narrative, her alternative discourse, which frees her from both Manuel's limited text and her familial text. Although she plans to return to Mexico, studying pre-Columbian literature and residing in Paris helps her to establish both temporal and geographic distance:

> It's not that I am fleeing from myself, but—how terrible—from the others, like my grandfather did. I am living my own basement experience in Paris, waiting for the best time to come out, like General Teodoro Leyva. . . .
>
> Perhaps I will never become the historian that I am seeking to be. Perhaps I cannot fly as far as I hope; but I will never stop trying. (155)

Dorotea thus ends on an inspirational note, making her an important role model in Mexican literature. She has managed to free herself from traditional bonds, and she has created her own alternative discourse, adding one more version to a multifaceted story. Thus, Molina has successfully written "beyond the ending." She has also managed to reparent herself, to re-create her childhood and herself as she would like to have been. "My mother and my grandmothers and my aunts and my sisters and my friends and I myself have been cowards," she explains, "and we fled from the adventure of finding ourselves at our very limits" (Molina, May 1990, 22). Molina's hope is that her daughters will lead a different life, while she will remake her life through literature:

> [I have tried] to fulfill my desires of pleasing myself with the fact that without being the woman I cannot be, [and being] the woman who is not given to living on the edge, the woman who hides in shyness and silence, I do not have to wait for the blow of the brutality of passion because I have suffered and

enjoyed it little by little in the life of writing. (Molina, May 1990, 22)

In her novel Molina also succeeds at questioning the authority of history. She has mixed photographs of historical figures and supposed photographs of her fictional characters, which are actually photos of her real relatives. In addition, she has used references to well-known historical texts, and to specific places and events, all of which create an impression of authenticity. Molina then undermines that very authenticity by playing with various levels and versions of fiction, alternately setting them up and tearing them down. The history books, the newspaper article, the general's diary, and even the narrator's own story are all questioned, all influenced by the god of cunning and deceit, all subject to creative alterations for personal, political or even playful reasons.

Historians and news writers may start with a set of verifiable facts, but then those facts are organized, some are eliminated, and they are given a meaning that the author forges. Therefore it is important to keep telling the other side of the story, because "there is no truth apart from the telling, no real story, no authorized version, no vantage point that allows experience to be viewed as a whole" (Hite 90). Ultimately it is the reader who must assimilate all versions of a story, creating his or her own version, and thus participating in the generation of meaning.

Three years after completing the first edition of La familia vino del norte, Molina once again employed metafiction and addressed the problem of the "official story" in her autobiographical novel Imagen de Héctor (image of Hector).

IMAGEN DE HÉCTOR

Each time that I looked at myself in the mirror, I had the impression that something of me was going to join with something else from those who had previously contemplated themselves in it. And I felt incomplete, as if each time I was losing the best of myself. There will come a day, I thought, in which there is nothing left of me. A day in which I am nothing but a solitary image suspended between a series of mirrors. I

> will exist in two dimensions, with no volume, furtively crossing the little planes of mercury.
>
> HÉCTOR PÉREZ MARTÍNEZ, IN
>
> *IMAGEN DE NADIE*

The tension between official and alternative discourse, history and fiction, and public and private images, is only one of many similarities between *La familia vino del norte* and *Imagen de Héctor*. The protagonist in both novels is a young woman searching for her identity by delving into her family's past, particularly that of one public figure. The families of both protagonists object to the investigation, and she must struggle against their opposition while trying to obtain information from them as well as from newspapers, books, family friends, and other sources. In both texts the present-day family is envisioned in a dream as artifacts from the past: in *La familia vino del norte* her family appears to her as mummies, and in *Imagen de Héctor* her family is the object of an archaeological search. The implication is that her family's ideas are antiquated, and she needs to decipher their messages in order to overcome them and formulate her own beliefs.

In both novels the author uses photographs of family members with historical figures, which augments the impression of authenticity. She also employs simple, direct language—pared down to the most essential syntax—in both texts. In *Imagen de Héctor* her language is almost infantile, particularly at the beginning of the book, as she mimics the thought processes of a young child. There is no definite resolution to the problem in either text; the struggle for self-realization advances, but must continue.

Molina has created alternative discourse in both texts, which consists of an alternative narrative structure, telling the other side of the story while not privileging a particular version as definitive, and writing beyond the ending. In both works she succeeds at writing beyond the ending by means of a transgressive narrative strategy called reparenting. In the first novel Molina is parenting a literary daughter, in the second she is parenting herself as a young girl. Therefore, she narrates in the first person in *La familia vino del norte* in order to create closeness with the woman she would like to become, and in *Imagen de Héctor* she uses the third person to create distance between herself and the young girl that she no longer wants to be.

In the earlier novel, Dorotea has a concrete discourse to oppose: Manuel's article, as well as her familial text and historical discourse. In contrast, the protagonist of the later novel investigates the life of Héctor Pérez Martínez, Molina's real father, who died when she was little more than one year old, and at first she has only myth, rumor, and faded memories to counteract. She is playing a solitary tennis game against a porous backboard: every time she hits the ball, it disappears into the mist. She needs to piece together a solid backboard so her balls will bounce back to her. This is her task, then: she needs to weave together and reconfirm memories, find information in the public record, and refer to Héctor's own books and papers in order to reconstruct the official image first, so that she can oppose it (or acknowledge it, assimilate it, deal with it, and surpass it).

Like *La familia vino del norte,* this later novel is metafiction: it is a story about how the protagonist/author gathered all the information, wrote it in her notebook, and transformed it into a narration that both assimilates the official discourse and creates an alternative one.

The problem with Héctor is that he had assumed mythical proportions. The protagonist, who is identified only as the Youngest Daughter, did not discover that he was dead until a neighbor boy told her, when she was five years old. Her family hid the truth from her by insisting that he was traveling and by maintaining many of his personal items in place. For the Youngest Daughter, Héctor was represented by his picture in the living room, a recording of his singing and playing the guitar, and some material objects strategically placed, awaiting his return: ties, glasses, pipes, and all of his clothing (in moth balls). In spite of this pervasive physical evidence, Héctor was still intangible. He became the mythical hero who, like Ulysses, would someday return home after a long and mysterious trip. He was remembered as the perfect father and husband, the best governor of Campeche and secretary of the interior, the best friend/writer/historian that anyone had ever known.

For the Youngest Daughter, the consequences are suffocating; she has a vague image of her father, whose memory has monstrous qualities rather than Prince Charming's ability to rescue fair damsels in distress:

> [It was] a world that closed in upon itself, that didn't allow anybody to leave, and it was beginning to asphyxiate her.
> Perhaps in Campeche—she thought—Héctor was suffering, a prisoner of pirates, since he didn't come to save her from that monster that lay in ambush for her everywhere.
> But Héctor didn't come back, he never finished his travels and came back. (13)[5]

The monster was Héctor's ghost, who smelled like moth balls and followed her around all day, attending her school ceremonies and interfering with her personal and academic progress. But the ghost is a memory she doesn't have, an image that she can't quite perceive, so she needs to paint his portrait for herself. When she sees her grandfather's photograph, she realizes that he looks just like her father, who in turn looks just like his son. This is one of her first clues to his identity, and her own:

> And the Youngest Daughter sensed that Héctor had also come to know himself in the old family portraits, confirming that he was made of bits and pieces of his ancestors like she was, she who felt so much anguish at not being able to find that portrait in which she ought to exist. (43–44)

The Youngest Daughter needs to recognize who her father really was, so that she can recognize herself and become somebody

---

[5] *All page numbers in this section, unless otherwise noted, are from* Imagen de Héctor *(Mexico City: Cal y Arena, 1990). All translations are mine, unless otherwise noted. Due to the length of this book, I have not included the original Spanish unless there is not a clear translation in English. The reader may refer back to the novel, using the page numbers provided.*

HISTORY AND HERSTORY

different, her own person. Molina, of course, is going through the same process as her protagonist, so she is attempting a kind of literary exorcism, for which the first step is to create distance between herself and her protagonist. The traditional distinctions between real author, implied author, narrator, and protagonist have been blurred in this text, so the author resorts to other strategies in order to create the distance necessary for the writing of this book. An obvious strategy is the use of capital letters to name the characters in relation to Héctor: Héctor's Mother, Héctor's Wife, the Older Sister, and so forth. The Youngest Daughter is never given a name, although many of the other characters are also called by their real-life names; Héctor's Wife is also called María Celis, and the Older Sister is named Dora, for example. This lack of a name creates distance; in the text, the author stops short of specifically identifying the protagonist with herself, in spite of having used the real names of her relatives, and in spite of her spoken declaration.[6] Thus she is free to invent and to reinvent her character.

There is also a tone that is sometimes reminiscent of children's writing, especially at the beginning of the novel. The story could almost open with the words "once upon a time there was a handsome prince named Héctor." This tone augments the temporal and emotional distance between the writer and her text.

In addition, Molina conveniently inserts an impersonal, unidentified narrator between herself and her protagonist. The narrator has no epic situation, that is, we are not told when or where the narrator is located as she tells the story. She also does not address a listener or a reader; she does not intrude upon the narration in any way, but she serves as a buffer between the author and the protagonist.

Molina's writing in this text is self-conscious metafiction. There is an obvious parallel between the Youngest Daughter's writing in her notebook and Molina's writing her novel. By describing the Youngest Daughter's reconstruction process, she also describes her own:

---

[6]*I am referring to her statement in the preceding interview, that the novel is autobiographical.*

SILVIA MOLINA

> The Youngest Daughter assembled and disassembled scenes with what she could find: the testimony of María Celis and the Older Children, the letters, the interviews with his friends, and the private papers which finally had emerged from the last boxes of a library that she had organized. (117)

The narrator establishes one more level of removal by creating conditional and contrary-to-fact statements: what the Youngest Daughter would have said to Héctor if she could (Why didn't you take care of yourself? Why did you work yourself to death?) and what the Youngest Daughter could have written in her notebook if she had so desired (a long history of his illness). The narrator reports the protagonist's hypothetical reproaches, as well as the lengthy documentation of Héctor's heart disease, which establishes a difference between the notebooks and the narration.

Another method of creating distance is to objectify Héctor, to make him an object of study. The narrator compares the Youngest Daughter's investigation to the study of a pre-Hispanic figure, and the protagonist has a dream in which her family's back yard is the site of an archaeological dig. The author also studies Héctor by reading the books that he wrote and quoting them in her own text. There is an interesting intertextual relationship between the father's and daughter's books on Campeche, and her novel. In 1940 Héctor published a book about his home state called *En los caminos de Campeche* (on the roads of Campeche), and in 1991 Molina published a collection of essays and other literature by natives of Campeche entitled *Campeche: Punta del ala del país* (Campeche: wingtip of the country) in which she reproduces much of her father's essay. This essay is also quoted and paraphrased in Molina's novel, but this time the subject of discourse is Héctor, not Campeche. The essay is quoted to reveal more about Héctor's character and thought patterns, not to publicize the problems that Campeche suffered in the late 1930s. Thus, Héctor's words are transformed by his daughter because she has transferred the focus from the state to the man.

The narrator also mentions by name the nine books that Héctor wrote in four years, which could send the reader back on a lengthy investigation, paralleling that of the Youngest Daughter. In addi-

HISTORY AND HERSTORY

tion, she quotes old newspaper articles, interviews with Héctor's friends, and Héctor's diary, which she exposes as another political document written for posterity, similar in that respect to the grandfather's diary in *La familia vino del norte*. Even though most of these sources present the official image of Héctor, she sorts through them carefully, trying to find insinuations of the real man. She also quotes the Youngest Daughter's notebook and a letter written by the protagonist to her former nanny, Miss Heidi. These last two documents were generated by Molina herself, in contrast to the other documents which are external to her text. The intertextual process creates distance and power for the protagonist, who assumes the ability to transform her father's words.

Distance is also created by the fragmentation of the protagonist. Rather than follow her progress chronologically through childhood to maturity, the narrator relies on a series of flashbacks, which depict the Youngest Daughter in various disconnected stages of development. The protagonist is seen as a young girl incapable of reading her father's books, and as a young woman finally able to comprehend. She also exists at some unidentified time later, the time of the narration:

> It would not be she, the Youngest Daughter, who would find out that the book that she had held in her hands, scarcely understanding it, had been written during Héctor's campaign for governor of the State in 1939.
>
> Only many years later, as a different person, the Youngest Daughter would find there the journalist of *El Nacional* (national news) making a series of chronicles about the isolation and poverty of a small town, and about the concrete problems that he had to confront as governor of Campeche from 1939 to 1943. (33)

The different identities of the Youngest Daughter are all remembered and presented by the narrator, as she fronts for the author, whose remembering is not mentioned. The bifurcation of time creates a juxtaposition of two different Youngest Daughters; one sits in the closet reading Héctor's books and looks up to see the other roaming the streets of Campeche in search of Héctor's memories. In contrast to her attempts to create a personal image of one man who progresses through time with the same identity in different circumstances, Molina creates for her alter ego, the Youngest Daughter, a series of selves, a portrait fractured into different time segments with different identities in each segment. Unity, integrity, and self-consistency are not privileged in this text, as they are in traditional narrative. As Molly Hite has commented, "To be whole by present-day standards is not to have resisted fragmentation but to have been reduced to a single fragment" (65). By that definition, being whole is not an advantage, it is a reduction. By means of this text, Molina has reconstructed one piece of her self; *La familia vino del norte* gave her other fragments as did previous works, and the process will continue, with the final result being a mosaic.

Accordingly, fragmentation is an important concept in Molina's alternative discourse, similar to the nonprivileging of a single truth, and it is emphasized by one of the elements in her alternative narrative structure that I have playfully labelled *temporal leapfrog*. For example, the present Youngest Daughter remembers sitting in the closet reading Héctor's books. The Youngest Daughter sitting in the closet remembers her trip to Campeche. While in Campeche, several people share memories of Héctor with her. Hop, hop, hop: the narrative moves back in time, changing focus and perspective, and creating an impression that is somewhat cinematographic. Another example of a series of temporal leaps is the scene in which the Youngest Daughter imagines Héctor lying in his hammock in Campeche, as he remembers the problems that have plagued his governorship. The hammock scene is interrupted by general descriptions of his activities as governor and by specific dialogues with friends and allies at different times in the past. The narrator often returns to Héctor in the hammock, who is smoking and stewing over his problems, unable to sleep. The section ends as María Celis joins her husband in the hammock to offer her tender consolation. The cinematographic elements of this section include the juxtaposition of public and private lives, the presentation of generalized, repetitive action punctuated by specific scenes, and the idealized love scene at the end. This is one of the problems that the protagonist is confronting: she sees her parents as having lived a Hollywood movie. How could her real, human self compete with that?

One of her self-defense tactics is the fragmentation of her self and the disassociation of the different fragments. She does not want to be Héctor's daughter any more; therefore she denies the continuum between Héctor's daughter and her self. She also creates multiple perspectives, and as Hite explains:

> The irresistible implication is that every perspective is as "correct" as every other perspective, and that the whole is constituted by all possible perspectives, and that therefore an apprehension of the whole is, strictly speaking, impossible. If fragmented perception is dangerous, the serious danger lies in mistaking a fragment for the truth in its entirety. (101)

Another self-defense mechanism is the humanization of the mythical figure of her father. Behind the polished, public image, the Youngest Daughter discovers an ambitious man who ruined his health and neglected his family and who covered up his true feelings in order to achieve political advancement. This very human Héctor had the unpretentious nickname of "Toto"; he stuttered; and he had a lover. None of these weaknesses disturb the Youngest Daughter; on the contrary, she is relieved to discover that Héctor was only human, as she is. Her sadness is obvious, however, as she slowly realizes the price that Héctor's family paid for his public life: "While Héctor had lived for others, his family had lost him little by little. The Youngest Daughter also became aware of the tremendous void that Héctor's absence had dug out in María Celis" (121).

The protagonist was essentially orphaned when her father died, leaving behind five children and a wife who subsisted on sleeping pills and denial. The Youngest Daughter, therefore, clings to Miss Heidi as a surrogate mother, and her inscription and amplification in the text is an important part of the reparenting strategy of the narrative. The importance of Miss Heidi in the protagonist's life has been intentionally exaggerated; in real life the nanny did not come back to get her after moving to London, and Molina did not visit her in Europe. Therefore, Molina has re-created a substitute parent for herself through her writing. She has also reparented herself by coming to terms with her mother's emotional absence and with her father's mythical and human images.

For Molina, this narrative is both an encounter and a "disencounter" *("desencuentro")*. She dedicates the book to her mother, and to "him, for the encounter that we had and we never planned." Nevertheless, the epilogue of the novel is called "The Disencounter," and she explains:

> What would Héctor say about the image of him that the Youngest Daughter had constructed?
> The Youngest Daughter thought about the ironic truth: without a doubt Héctor would have asked himself who the Youngest Daughter was, since he never managed to know her. (149–50)

In other words, the protagonist has succeeded in discovering the human side of her father, thus demystifying his image and creating a parental figure with which she can coexist. However, she was not able to re-create a flesh-and-blood father for herself; she cannot really have a filial relationship with the figure that she has re-created. Earlier in the novel, the narrator quotes Héctor's autobiographical essay *Imagen de nadie* (image of nobody), in which he laments that he is the sum total of all of his ancestors, and he would prefer to be something different (64–65). Molina has managed to replace "nobody" with "Héctor," in the title of her book, and for herself. She has also realized that she, too, is the sum total of all those who have come before her, and that knowledge has set her free. Perhaps in a subsequent novel she will replace the "Youngest Daughter" with a character who has a name and an individual identity.

Both of Molina's novels studied here demonstrate the use of literary discourse as personal therapy, and in that sense they are quite different from Elena Poniatowska's collective outcry and Angeles Mastretta's sassy contradiction of the official story. They are similar in function, however, to the novels of the American writer Barbara Kingsolver, particularly her work *Animal Dreams,* in which a young woman returns to her home town to confront her family's past and her own identity. One obvious difference is that in *Animal Dreams* love and quest are not mutually exclusive. Even though Molina has stated that the solution will be the couple,[7] in *La familia vino del norte* Dorotea's quest is facilitated by her rupture with family and lovers, and in *Imagen de Héctor* the quest is solitary from beginning to end. Kingsolver's protagonist, in contrast, manages to resolve her family conflicts, find her true professional calling, and fall in love with a supportive male. This might be too much for the modern reader to believe, but on the other hand, judging by the direction that Molina's life and prose have taken, it just could be the plot for her next novel.

But as I am blithely predicting her next protagonist and plot, I cannot forget what Molina has already achieved, laying the groundwork for such projections. In these two novels she has created an alternative discourse that consists of an alternative narrative structure (including temporal leapfrog, imbedding of texts, and intertextuality with texts both internal and external to her fictional space) as well as an alternative ideology and plot line. The latter refers to her telling the other side of the story by presenting multiple perspectives with no privileged truth, and writing beyond the ending by creating new choices for her protagonist and opportunities for reparenting. In contrast to Elena Poniatowska's justifiably strident rejection of the official discourse and Angeles Mastretta's mocking disregard for it, Silvia Molina has presented an official discourse that she does not reject or mock; she simply modifies it with love and careful research, creating an image that is more human, a more solid backboard for her solitary tennis game.

---

[7]*She said this in the preceding interview.*

PART IV
BRIANDA DOMECQ

Chapter Ten
Introduction

"You are going to be a writer,"
[my grandmother] said to me,
without even bothering
to explain what that was
or if it was good or bad;
and the next day she gave me
my first notebook
and a new, sharpened pencil.
It was then that I started to write
and I discovered the road
and the escape
that in some way
has permitted me to survive.

BRIANDA DOMECQ,
BD: DE CUERPO ENTERO[1]

Some authors choose to write, others do it for economic or professional reasons, and then there are those like Brianda Domecq who are born to write. For them, writing becomes an obligation, an obsession, a force that leads them through life. Referring to the traditional *cantadoras*[2] (storytellers) who preserve women's oral history, Clarissa Pinkola Estés explains in Women Who Run with the Wolves: "For the most part, we tell stories when we are summoned by them, and not vice versa" (462). As a cantadora who writes, Brianda has been summoned by each of her stories, sometimes quite forcefully. Her first novel, *Once días . . . y algo más* (eleven days . . . and even more) (1979), is a chronicle of her experience when she was kidnapped and held prisoner in November 1978. The story was something that had to be written in order for her to understand and process what happened to her, and to her captors. Her novel reveals the human connections that were made between the kidnappers and their victim during eleven very tense days and nights, when the survival of each person involved depended upon the actions of everyone else. This novel goes way beyond a simple crime story, to reveal the thoughts, fears, personality, and character development of each individual. In contrast to well-known crime stories such as *Crime and Punishment, The Executioner's Song,* and *In Cold Blood,* Brianda's novel is narrated in the first-person singular, in the present tense, and from the victim's point of view. In spite of this perspective, the criminals are presented as complex human beings, with their own foibles, insecurities, and compassion for others.

The subject of Brianda's next novel, *La insólita historia de la*

---

[1] *The translation of the epigraph is mine, as are all other translations in this part.*
[2] *Estés uses a form that derives from cantar (to sing), rather than from contar (to tell). This may be intentional; if not, it is an interesting slip.*

BRIANDA DOMECQ

Santa de Cabora (the unusual story of the saint from Cabora), published in 1990, summoned her in a less obvious but more seductive manner. She first discovered the existence of her protagonist, Teresa Urrea, upon reading Heriberto Frías' book *Tomóchic,* a novel about the late nineteenth-century massacre of all of the inhabitants of the town of Tomóchic, by federal troops sent by the dictator Porfirio Díaz. The rebellious leaders of Tomóchic had chosen Teresa Urrea to be their patron saint, just as the insurgents in the war of independence from Spain in 1810 had taken a banner of the Virgin of Guadalupe to be their flag and their inspiration. Because of Teresa's miraculous cures and her message of social reform, her fame spread throughout Mexico until Porfirio Díaz deemed it necessary to exile her to the United States. In the cold, unreceptive climate of this country, Teresa's powers and fame languished, and her memory faded out of existence. Brianda Domecq's calling, then, was to rescue this remarkable woman from oblivion. The travels, interviews, and detailed research necessary for the creation of this complex historical novel took over Brianda's life for seventeen years.

That kind of obsession is contagious. The first time I met Brianda, she had called me on her cellular phone from the street outside my apartment building in Mexico City. As I climbed into the car, her first words to me were, "I'm going to kidnap you!" And she did. I had carefully chosen a restaurant for the interview—I had even located a nearby parking lot—but all of my arrangements were ignored. I let Brianda choose a place, so that she could feel safe, because I suspected that the lessons learned from her kidnapping ordeal were engraved in her mind. She took me to an elegant restaurant and treated me to the best meal I've ever had in Mexico City. During the meal, Brianda used that sinister verb "kidnap" over and over again until it was bereft of meaning and emptied of pain. She wished to share her ordeal, to kidnap me as she was kidnapped, and to obsess me as she was obsessed with Teresa. And she succeeded. I had never seen this woman before, but for a few short hours that day and the next, we were best friends.

Our first interview took place in Brianda's car, because the restaurant's loud music prevented me from taping. We were on

INTRODUCTION

our way to a lecture at the *Colegio de México,* and Brianda wove expertly through the heavy rain and the frenzied traffic, braking and accelerating as necessary, barely pausing in her detailed answer as we were almost sideswiped by a truck. Brianda is an attractive, slender woman of medium height, with blue eyes and short blond hair, casually coiffed. She looked relaxed in slacks and a sweater, her lack of pretension belying the prestige of her family. Her father was Pedro Domecq, the famous entrepreneur of *Casa Domecq,* producer of brandy and fine wines. After our second meeting she hugged and kissed me when we parted. She and I had connected, we had touched each other, and I experienced in person Brianda's amazing capacity to forge human bonds.

Brianda was born on 1 August 1942, in New York City. Her father was Pedro Domecq González, Viscount of Almocadén, Knight of Calatrava, and black sheep of his wine-producing Spanish family. Her mother was Elizabeth Cook, of New York. Somehow this mixture of Spanish, Moorish, French, English, German, Jewish, and Irish blood produced a mischievous little girl with infinite curiosity. Brianda was named for a woman who took up her husband's sword after his death and led a battle against the Moors at Jerez de la Frontera, Spain, in the fifteenth century. Brianda lived in New York City until she was five, when her family moved to a farm in Connecticut. Like Elena Poniatowska, she moved to Mexico at the age of nine. Her father's wine-producing business in Mexico was so successful that it was necessary for the family to move to Mexico City. The adjustment to a new language and country was difficult for Brianda, and she went through an extended period of adolescent rebellion. She returned to the United States for two years of boarding school and one year of college, so for a long time she was divided between two cultures. As an adult, she has assumed her Mexican identity, and although she is still bilingual, her professional writing is all in Spanish.[3]

The reviews of Brianda's writing have generally been fa-

---

[3]*Most of this information is included in BD: De cuerpo entero.*

vorable in Mexico, with one notable exception,[4] and she has gained the attention of the respected author and critic John Brushwood, who published a commendatory review of *Once días . . . y algo más* in Mexico City's *El Universal*. In a review for the same newspaper, Antonio Acevedo Escobedo pointed out Brianda's originality, sincerity, and uncommon description of emotions and sensations in her first novel, and Jorge Munguía Espitia has called her second work "an outstanding novel that is worthwhile reading" (62). Another Mexican critic, Rafael Solana, recently gave Brianda's second novel very high praise in the magazine *Siempre*. However, there have been few analytical articles and no books published on Brianda's work, and only a few of her short stories have been translated into English.[5] Part of the problem is the lack of publicity and distribution of her books, because it is hard to find her novels even in Mexico City.

Brianda received her degree in Hispanic language and literature from the National Autonomous University of Mexico (UNAM), and did one year of graduate study at the prestigious *Colegio de México* in Mexico City. She was editor in chief of the *Revista de Bellas Artes* (fine arts magazine) in 1973, and from 1983 to 1985 she was president of PRONATURA (a Mexican conservation association). Because of her and her husband's hard work, and the fact that her two children are adults, she now has the luxury of being a full-time writer, but that has not always been the case. She and her husband, Fernando Rodríguez, lived for a long time on his income as a radiologist, and Brianda spent years working as a translator and publicity writer. Although the Mexican public—including the kidnappers—believes the Domecq family to be enormously wealthy, that simply is not true. When Brianda's father died, her entire inheritance consisted of one very old pair of binoculars.

Becoming a creative writer has been a struggle for Brianda, as it has been for all of the women authors of her generation. She explains:

---

[4] Miguel Angel Morales, writing for the *Excélsior* in Mexico City, published a scathing review of *Once días . . . y algo más*. (See the Works Cited.) His criticism is more vitriolic than analytical, however, and he appears to have a personal grudge against Brianda.

[5] I am solving this problem by translating her novels myself.

INTRODUCTION

> [We are just beginning to acquire] courage: the courage to say what we think and to accept the consequences; the courage to confront the unavoidable solitude that results when a woman acts and speaks with sincerity in this society that is still patriarchal; the courage to confront reality directly, in spite of the masculine figures that guard the doors of our lives (father, brother, husband, son, priest). (January 1990, 9)

In addition to the two above-mentioned novels, Brianda has published a collection of short stories called *Bestiario Doméstico* (domestic bestiary), in which there is an outstanding trilogy of stories that rewrite the myth of creation to include an archetypal feminist.[6] She has also written a book-length essay about the Río Grande and a brief autobiography that is part of a series called *De cuerpo entero* (in full view). Her anthology *Acechando al unicornio: la virginidad en la literatura mexicana* (stalking the unicorn: virginity in Mexican literature) includes a lengthy prologue that explores the theme of virginity in four centuries of Mexican writing. She has just completed a collection of essays on Mexican women writers, entitled *Mujer que publica, mujer pública* (woman of words, woman of the streets).

Brianda's studies and work as an anthologist have made her acutely aware of the lack of a literary tradition for women writers in Mexico. Although there have been a few stars in four centuries of darkness, contemporary Mexican women authors are currently creating their own tradition, as Brianda affirms:

> We are setting precedents; our literary daughters and granddaughters will not have to start at ground zero: they will have our works—the good, the mediocre, and the bad ones—as a school where they can learn tomorrow from our achievements and mistakes. This is fundamental and I feel very proud to be a part of it. (January 1990, 9)

Brianda's books offer more than just literary lessons. They offer life stories, the tales of women who survive, who struggle, who

---

[6] *I plan to include a translation of this trilogy in an anthology of short stories by Mexican women writers.*

somehow manage to shape their own destiny. Brianda's protagonists are strong women, and they are women who have connected with others to form ephemeral or lasting alliances. In that sense, they offer another dimension to the solitary quest personified by Silvia Molina's characters. Just as Brianda's protagonists connect with other characters, she connects with other people, discovering strength in solidarity as well as within herself.

CHAPTER ELEVEN

Interview
Brianda Domecq

KG: How did you begin to write, and what was your inspiration?[1]

BD: I feel that my vocation is the result of a possibility and a process. I remember two things from my childhood in respect to this question: my father taught me the power of imagination to alleviate suffering, since he told me stories at night when I was afraid. He was also the one who taught me how to penetrate fiction in order to transform it with my own life, because the two of us invented and acted out stories as we walked through the woods. Later this process was inverted as I learned to transform life into fiction in order to understand life or give it a meaning. Thus my childhood, like that of literature itself, was full of oral tradition. Even though it served me then as a means of escape, now it has become a vital commitment to understanding life.

I remember that my grandmother used to tell me that I should be a writer, perhaps because I talked so much. She realized that I had ideas and preoccupations that needed to be channeled in a constructive way. My grandmother had a lot of common sense—the least common of the senses—and she intuited truths that she relayed as maxims, which would have been difficult for her to explain. With time, I have been able to understand and to utilize that same capacity of knowing something without having to pass through the rational and logical process of "masculine" thought, and I have confirmed how wise she was with her intuitions.

Finally, my father was a frustrated writer. He always said that he wanted to be a writer but his family forced him to be an engineer, and life forced him to be a merchant. At the end of his life he tried to write his memoirs, but he discovered that writing isn't just having something to say; you also have to know how to say it, you have to learn the trade.

I remember that I started writing very early, at about ten years of age. In school, when they asked for a composition in history class, for example, I made up a story that took place in the period we were studying. I wrote things in a notebook; I

---

[1] *This interview is based on two conversations that I had with Brianda in August 1992.*

INTERVIEW

loved to write letters, and during adolescence I wrote poems. Without a doubt the possibility of being a writer was already within me, and I know that in some vague way I also had the desire. However, I still needed to go through the long process of learning how to write, which I didn't undertake until I was married, with two children. Since I had to stay home taking care of children, I signed up for a correspondence course called "Famous Writer's School," and I started writing stories in English and sending them to magazines in the United States. I wrote a lot in two years, but I only managed to publish one story in a little-known American magazine. I remember that they paid me eighty dollars, and I thought it was fantastic. But the numerous failures convinced me that the world wasn't waiting to discover me and that becoming a writer would require more than infantile dreams and desires.

When my younger child started kindergarten, I started studying literature at the university and I began to write in Spanish. Before that I had worked as a copyeditor in an advertising agency, and I had done translations from English to Spanish for two years. Both jobs had helped me learn the basics of written Spanish, that is, they had encouraged me to change from my maternal language to my paternal language as a tool of the trade. During my university studies I learned more about writing, by studying and analyzing the work of the masters. I started writing and publishing in Spanish: poems, essays, and short stories. I attended several writing workshops, and I was completely devoted to learning the trade. The kidnapping that I endured gave me the opportunity to write my first long text, which could be called a nonfiction novel, since the content is autobiographical, but the structure is that of a novel.

KG: What precursors do you have, and what other influences have there been on your work?

BD: This kind of question has always worried me; it triggers my "blank mind syndrome." I believe that the question of precursors and influences is masculine; it is more relevant to the writers who are worried about fitting into a school, into some "ism"; [they are worried] about being in the vanguard, and separating from a tradition in order to do something innovative. Many times, after drawing a blank on this question, I have told myself that I should be disciplined and I should look for or invent "influences" so that I could respond the next time, but that doesn't work for me. To tell the truth, it doesn't interest me. What I feel is that everything that I have read has left a sediment in me, a literary sediment from which ideas or solutions come forth when I am working on a text, without those ideas being attached to any label or source. Afterwards, it is possible that I will discover the origin of something that I have included in a text; for example, the use of the zodiac signs for names in *Once días . . . y algo más* (eleven days . . . and even more) probably comes from Norman Mailer's use of Aquarius as the narrator's name in *Of a Fire on the Moon,* which I translated. Sometimes a critic will point out an influence to me, like the use of the leitmotif in *La insólita historia de la Santa de Cabora* (the unusual story of the saint from Cabora), which is reminiscent of García Márquez.[2] But all of that, for me, is a function of the unconscious mind, which participates in the act of writing. Perhaps the explanation is that I live apart from the literary world. My areas of action and interest have had more to do with the worlds of psychology, feminism, and ecology. In that sense I am interested in writing literature that is not about literature, but about life.

KG: Do you believe that your contact with two cultures has increased your narrative possibilities?

BD: I think that is possible, because each culture is a vision of the world, each language is a vision of the world, and obviously North American literature is not the same as Mexican literature. Thus, a mixture of the two could emerge from what I call my literary sediment, creating new and interesting combinations.

KG: How were you affected by the massacre of 1968?

BD: I was very much apart from that world, also. I found out

---

[2]*She is referring to the manner in which each chapter begins—"On the day of her second death Teresa would remember . . ."—which is reminiscent of the chapter openings in Gabriel García Márquez's* One Hundred Years of Solitude.

INTERVIEW

about and reacted to [that event] like just another spectator. I didn't enter the university until 1972. In 1968 I was married, with two small children, and I was in psychoanalysis because of an existential crisis. In order to pay for my psychoanalysis I took a job as a typist for the Olympic Committee and it was there that I learned about the student movement. In fact, the offices were on University Avenue, and I was working there the night that the tanks passed by to take over the university. I saw everything as a spectator, with all the contradictory emotions that everybody experienced during those times. I have never been interested in politics. When I was at the university I was interested for a while in leftist ideas, but ideologies of all leanings have always bothered me. I consider them a manipulation, and I have always believed that if you scratch the surface of any ideology—whether it be leftist, rightist, or even feminist—you will find the old patriarchal structure which has encumbered us all for such a long time (even though it had its necessity and its purpose). I have little use for structured faith, and every ideology—like every religion—demands faith from its followers, not only in the human spirit but also in the letter of the law that the ideology has structured.

KG: Do you consider yourself a feminist or a humanist?
BD: My answer to that is related to my attitude toward ideologies. Yes, I consider myself a feminist, but not a militant; in other words, my feminism is a search, not a political position. And yes, I also consider myself a humanist because I have always understood feminism as a neohumanism in that it attempts to subvert at its base the patriarchal system that has stolen humanity from all of us, men and women alike. What is fascinating about feminism is the possibility of defining women not as women but as human beings. The definition of a human being has always been equivalent to the definition of man; women have always been relegated to the margin, lumped together as something called Woman, which is more a myth than a reality. Now we are fighting to have access to all the possibilities of a human being, and to incorporate into the

concept of human being that which is feminine, heretofore consigned to oblivion by the patriarchy.

After my kidnapping, when I was asked what it had meant to me, I remember repeating many times that it had been a profoundly human experience. Many people interpreted that as meaning that I had enjoyed it. No, no, no, what is human includes both joy and suffering, and in that sense it was an experience that touched the essence of being human.

KG: How did your kidnapping affect your life, your writing, and your thought with regard to Mexico?

BD: My thoughts about Mexico did not change at all, because the kidnapping did not have anything to do with politics. It was like a robbery: you steal something and then you sell it to the highest bidder. As for my life, I think it was a time of deep self-analysis, both during and after the kidnapping; the experience made me realize the essential human values: the touch of a hand, tenderness, communication, shared moments. That is, the necessity of human relationships, of honesty, in that sense it was like being in a pressure cooker in which I was forced to do without everything external, superfluous, all the superficial values of life, like the car one has or the way one dresses. I had to rely on what was absolutely essential: daily survival, living completely in the present because the past was out of reach and the future was totally unknown from moment to moment. It was a shock to go back to what is fundamental: emotional and mental needs, physical needs like eating and bathing. Suddenly everything was so simplified and I was under so much pressure that only the essential things were viable.

As for my writing, well, that was a big jolt because for the first time I dared to write a novel. I had published stories, essays, and poems, but I had never embarked upon a lengthy text, and I was terrified of trying. I was convinced that I would probably just write short stories all of my life, because writing a novel seemed too big a project. But the kidnapping story was something that I absolutely had to write, so that was like my first class on writing, on how to structure a novel, how to create a narrative voice. That book had four versions before the final version was published. I tried telling it many different

INTERVIEW

ways. First I tried telling it in the first person, but that didn't work; then I tried a strange experiment in the second person, using the *tú* form [the familiar form of *you*]; then I tried the third person, and I tried using the present tense and the past tense. Each version dried up on me, but nevertheless they each left something, and the final version has both first and second person [and the epilogue is narrated in the third person]. There is a division in the protagonist's mind sometimes, as she speaks to herself, saying, "You, be quiet" and "Don't say that" or "What are you doing?" And the story is told in the present tense, but using minimal flashbacks, when the narration skips a morning, for example, and then the events of that morning are told in the immediate past.

KG: Was writing *Once días . . . y algo más* a way for you to explain what happened, to yourself as well as to your family and the public?

BD: I think that it began with my need to understand it myself. Afterwards I received a letter from Vicente Leñero[3] in which he said that it is very difficult to write a story when you know how it ends. I think that wasn't the difficult part, but rather it was writing a story when one is still not conscious of the meaning of the story, which in my case was a profound human relationship, no matter how strange that might seem. It was the emergence of essential human values among six human beings who shared eleven days in a very strange and extreme situation. It was something that just happened—the closeness that we felt—and I didn't know anything about the Stockholm syndrome,[4] which was brought up afterwards in reference to Patty Hearst.[5] When I

---

[3] *Vicente Leñero (1933–), born in Guadalajara, Mexico, is a well-known writer. His works include* Los albañiles *(the bricklayers),* El evangelio de Lucas Gavilán *(the gospel of Lucas Gavilan), and* Pueblo rechazado *(rejected people).*

[4] *The Stockholm syndrome is the psychological term for the emotional bond that sometimes develops between captives and captors.*

[5] *Patricia Hearst, the daughter of the newspaper publisher Randolph Hearst, was kidnapped in 1974 by the Symbionese Liberation Army. She assumed a new name and identity, and began to participate in some of the illegal activities of her captors, including a bank robbery. She and her kidnappers were captured by the police, and she served three years in prison.*

read about the syndrome afterwards I realized that this was precisely what happened, there is a dependence on and therefore a gratitude [toward the kidnappers]. I can interpret it in a psychoanalytical way: there is a regression, one is in the position of a baby, very dependant upon other people. And if those people don't feed the baby, it dies; and the kidnapped person is in the same situation. There is total dependance, your life is in the hands of other people, and if your basic needs are satisfied this obviously produces gratitude—which in a baby is expressed as love and a need for its parents—and a very strong bond. I didn't understand that when I first started writing the book. That is the psychoanalytical explanation, but apart from that vision there was a communication, a humanization of the kidnappers as well as the protagonist. As the novel develops, they all become more human, more essential, their values become more evident. I love the scene in which they exchange recipes, and the exercise scene. Everything is so basic, and the kidnappers begin expressing their needs, too, with the protagonist, with me. And thus bonds are formed; it's like transference in psychoanalysis, but it's more profound, like love between parents and children, which emerges from this absolute necessity that one feels for the other.

KG: How much of the novel is based on reality?

BD: The novel is almost 100 percent reality, but the structure is novelistic. I believe that I hardly made up anything; I changed the details of the place, I polished, I augmented, I added conversations, but what takes place in the novel actually happened. It's just novelized.

KG: Did you keep a diary, or how did you remember so many details?

BD: I think that I remembered so many details because the experience was so intense. Obviously, I didn't write a diary during the time I was kidnapped. Afterwards, I wrote a very lengthy diary; it was almost like therapy. I wrote down all my memories and also everything that was going on after the kidnapping, all the disagreeable things: the police, going to identify the kidnappers, the lies, all the filth of the world, which—as strange as it may seem—was not in that room where I was held prisoner. The filth of the world was present in the character of the boss, the one who was making the deal. But the rest were apart from all that, in spite of their participation in the kidnapping. I never read that diary again, but it served to organize my thoughts, and then I wrote them over and over again. So yes, there are things that I invented, but the novel is fundamentally autobiographical. I mean, you don't have to elaborate on reality if reality writes the book.

KG: Is it true that your husband understood your feelings after the kidnapping?

BD: I believe so. He had the help of a friend of ours who is a psychoanalyst. This friend went immediately to our house and he was there with him for several days, because it was a situation of terrible anguish. My family didn't know if I was dead or alive, or what they were doing to me, if they were taking care of me, if they were raping me, how horrible! So it was a little hard for him to understand this absolute bond that I had with the kidnappers, and why I cried so much. One day our whole family went to the beach to rest because every morning I got up and I cried and cried. I saw a sunset and I cried, everything made me cry. So he said to me that day, "I hope that some day you can love me as much as you love the kidnappers." I said, "It isn't that. You're wrong. It's a strange bond; it hurts me a lot, I feel as though someone I cherish has died, but it isn't love." I still hadn't written my book, and I still didn't understand everything. He was very patient with me; the recuperation period was very long. But my husband is a very understanding man. We have been through a lot together: we were each in psychoanalysis, and then we were in analysis together, as a couple. We have grown a lot together, and that has allowed for greater patience, tranquility, comprehension, and communication than what the average couple would have. Or maybe it's like that for other people, too; it's just that I feel it more, and I love him a lot. But there wasn't a whole lot to understand; everything was a given and there was no way to change what happened.

What I feared—and this comes out in the book—was that the family and especially my husband would take a vengeful attitude, one of resentment and paranoia. But that didn't happen. He was afraid afterwards; he put telephones in our cars and for a long time I always called when I was going out or coming back from some place. But he was alright. He even felt the same kind of bond with the boss, with whom he communicated during the kidnapping. He felt like the boss was the only friend in the world who could tell him how his wife was. That was what I wanted to show in the book: those human bonds, those emotions, those ties between the kidnappers and the person kidnapped.

KG: The reader experiences those same bonds. After reading your book I felt like I had been through all of that, too.

BD: That is precisely what I wanted to do; I wanted to kidnap the reader, to put him/her in that room in contact with the kidnappers, and to make him/her feel all of those emotions. In daily life we tend to obscure the emotions, they are not useful to us. We have to manage things intellectually, but in a situation like that, the emotions come forward: sadness, fear, the sense of loss. I had never felt fear like that; it was horrendous. But my problem was how to get the reader into the room with me; that's why I wrote in the present tense, to create suspense, even though the end was evident because the author is obviously writing the book.

KG: Even though I haven't had the same experience as you did, your novel helped me to rethink the trauma in my own life. I felt encouraged by the way you managed to survive that incredible ordeal.

BD: In that sense it is equivalent to any critical situation in which there is a real threat. One of the fascinating things was the mental split in which there was an observer inside of me. There was a person living the experience, but there was another person observing it and saying, "How are you going to act in the face of death? How are you going to deal with fear? How are you going to react to aggression?" Just like the thoughts of any young man who is sent to war: "How are you going to act on the battlefield? How are you going to act in an extreme situation?" You never know until you are there, until you are submerged in a situation where all you can do is face

INTERVIEW

it. That is one of the existential questions, how would a human being act, how would I act, because everyone reacts differently. I have a friend who was carrying a six-pack of beer in her hand when some jerks tried to kidnap her, and she hit them with the six-pack, and she got away. So her reaction was aggressive, she defended herself physically. My reaction was to not move a finger, so they wouldn't stick that knife in me.

The most difficult part was telling a story in which nothing happens, because nothing really happens. Also, wanting to put the reader in the room implied the use of the present tense and the first person, which can be boring as narrative techniques. So that was the greatest challenge: writing and structuring the story so that it would be exciting, so the reader would feel kidnapped, without resorting to a confessional mode.

KG: Sometimes when you criticized yourself, I thought, "Don't criticize yourself! You are suffering so much, and then to mortify yourself, too, that's too much torture!"

BD: Well, that's the superego. I am terribly demanding with myself, and being so critical has cost me a lot in terms of self-esteem and self-confidence. Now I am learning not to be so critical, to accept myself more. I am what I am and that's it; after fifty years I'm not going to change much.

KG: Did you ever see the kidnappers again?

BD: Yes, of course, [the one I called] the *Pícaro* (the Rascal) followed me afterwards. The day after I was rescued I told my husband, "I have to go out, because it's like I fell off a horse, and if I don't get back up on the horse right now, I won't ever ride again. I have to go out alone; I'm going to the market." So he told me to take his beeper, even though you couldn't talk on it, it just made beeping noises. And he said that if anything strange happened, I should pretend to be talking into the beeper. So I went to the market alone and there I saw a dark-skinned man with straight hair who was pushing a cart, and every time I entered one of the aisles, he entered the same aisle from the other end. He kept looking at me, and I started to panic. The boss promised to have me killed if I said anything, and I thought this was it. I went to another aisle, and the man appeared at the other end again. At the time I didn't know who had escaped, and I thought it was probably [the one I called] Santa Claus, not the *Pícaro*. So I took out the gadget that [my husband] Fernando had given me and I pretended to talk into it. The man disappeared immediately and I looked for the store manager and they searched for him but they never found him. Afterwards I found out that it was the *Pícaro*, because he was the one who escaped and it was logical that he would follow me. I felt very sorry because if I had known that it was the *Pícaro* I would have spoken to him, I swear I would have spoken to him.

KG: And you never saw him again?

BD: No, never. The others were given forty years in jail, and he must have thought, "This is the end." But I had never seen him, and he didn't say "Pst." If he had said "Pst" I would have realized who he was, but he didn't identify himself in any way; I suppose he was afraid. He didn't know what I was carrying, but he knew I was alone because he must have followed me. Afterwards I heard that the boss was killed in jail. He probably was doing one of his dirty deals, manipulating people and forming his gang, and somebody shot him in jail.

KG: Are the others still in jail?

BD: They probably are out by now. The wives of the Bartender and Santa Claus came to ask me to please do something to get them out of jail, but what could I do? That's life; they committed a crime.

KG: Is your novel *La insólita historia de la Santa de Cabora* also autobiographical?

BD: All the literature that I write is somewhat autobiographical; my writing originates from an identification with a character or a situation. In fact, Teresita (the saint from Cabora) got inside me. I didn't invite her; I found her in a book and she possessed me, she installed herself inside me and there she was for seventeen years. She seems to be more tranquil now that I have finished her book. That's why I say that there is so much that is unconscious in the process of creating literature. After writing the novel I saw very definite coincidences between Teresa's life and mine. First, Teresita is an illegitimate daughter and I am the daughter of my father's

INTERVIEW

second marriage, so in Spain I am considered illegitimate because my father never divorced his first wife, since he was eighty years old when divorce was legalized. I also can identify the figure of [the folk healer] Huila with my own grandmother, who was one of my teachers. The relationship between Don Tomás and Teresa is similar to my relationship with my father. In addition, I was able to imitate the accent of the people from the north [of Mexico] because I married a northerner, and I have visited that region often. My husband's family is a typical ranch family from Sonora. So there are many aspects that coincide with my own life, but I think that it is also autobiographical in an internal way. The search for meaning in her life—Teresa's desperate wish to know the origin of her powers, what they mean, what they are good for—all of that existential questioning is not specifically mine, but I have experienced it and I think that it is universal. It is human, after all. So in that sense it is autobiographical, but I think many of the connections were inadvertent.

KG: Did you really go to Cabora?

BD: Yes.

KG: Did you talk with Teresa's relatives?

BD: Yes, that part is also true. The role of the investigator is mainly autobiographical. Obviously, it is exaggerated to enhance its dramatic function and to present a question that Teresa asks herself: she feels responsible for many deaths. As she says, by trying to give life it seems like I am sowing death. So the question is, did Teresa really take over the investigator's life so that she could tell her story? That is the game of the double, the bifurcated life. That's why the investigator doesn't have a name, or a story; she is really a human being occupied by another human being, and living the life of the other person.

KG: How much do you believe in the miracles that Teresa performed?

BD: I am a great believer in miracles for the simple reason that life is a miracle and everything that happens is a miracle. I especially believe in everyday miracles. I think my life is a miracle; every day things happen that are miraculous. Your wanting to write about my work is a miracle. I think I believe in miracles; it depends on what you mean by believe. If you want to know if she healed people, well, I think that she did. But, how? One can cure by the power of suggestion, or by emanations, vibrations, or special energy in the hands. Apparently, Teresa had an innate capacity to hypnotize, and that can explain a lot of her ability to relieve pain instantly or to make a person sleep and then wake up and feel cured. But as it says in the epigraph [of my novel], since I am agnostic I can imagine many possibilities. But frankly, I don't feel capable of giving an answer like "no, I don't believe" or "yes, I believe." I prefer to leave doubt, and I think that I do that in the novel. The reader has to decide, or not decide, just be satisfied with the idea that this happened, but who knows how or why it happened.

KG: How do you think Teresa's powers were affected by her persecution and exile?

BD: I think that as she goes further and further away from her homeland, she becomes a public spectacle and she comes in contact with a public that doesn't believe, and that is why her powers are diminished. Magic is something that is produced not only in the person, but in the environment. It is like a hero who is not born a hero, but he becomes a hero because of circumstances. The environment can transform a normal act into an abnormal one.

KG: Did you make up Teresa's genealogy that you presented in the *Introito* (introit, or introductory prayer)?

BD: Yes. It is obviously taken from the genealogy of Jesus, but the names are invented, except for Cayetana, Teresa's mother, and the names are all of women. This feminine genealogy is interesting because in the work of women writers I am finding more and more mention of the need to recuperate feminine lineage, because under patriarchy women lose their name, their lineage, everything. So there is a hunger for genealogy.

KG: When the investigator forgets her portfolio, it seems that she is entering a new stage of her investigation, in which she is going to live Teresa's life instead of studying it. Am I right?

BD: I believe so. The loss of the portfolio is the turning point, when she enters a kind of ecstasy; she swallows Teresa, because

INTERVIEW

she carries the documents inside her. From that point on, her alienation from herself and her possession by Teresa continue in crescendo until she falls down the hill. Besides, there is something symbolic about the loss of the documents, which permits Teresa to live, because the history is lost; what is on the register is lost. That didn't really happen—obviously I still have the documents—but that was a literary element that I wanted to include there.

KG: Do you think that this intense identification with the person you are studying is something new, something that women can contribute to history and to literature?

BD: Not especially. That would be a dangerous assertion. Perhaps what you perceive is the point of view that a woman writer takes, which is sometimes more internal. That is, we are more interested in the interior of a person than the historical events. But I don't think that this is a woman's prerogative. For example, in *Madero el otro* (the other Madero), [the author] Ignacio Solares is completely identified with [Francisco] Madero, he is totally inside Madero. I think the difference is between a person who decides to write a novel about a certain historical figure, and a person who is haunted by a character as Ignacio Solares was, as I was.

KG: Then what do you think women can contribute to literature and to historical investigation?

BD: I think they can contribute a different vision of the world. I think that biology influences one's existential vision; life takes on different meaning and perspective when one can conceive and give birth than when one cannot. Women's biological function definitely gives us experiences that are totally denied to men. Also, I believe that the marginalized social position of women allows us to present events from a different perspective, which I would call tangential. For the first time we are seeing the perspective of the other half of humanity; women are talking about their own eroticism, their own bodies, the experience of virginity, of menstruation, of maternity, and they are deconstructing the old myths. Even though they may be creating new myths, that doesn't matter, at least they are different.

KG: Going back to your novel, to what extent do you think that [your protagonist] Teresa has failed?

BD: I think that the concept of success as we understand it now is a patriarchal concept, and according to this patriarchal concept Teresa failed completely. She was defeated by "evil," she was exiled, she was separated from everything that was hers. Nonetheless, from an existential point of view I think that Teresa succeeded because she was capable of progressively understanding things, of growing with her experiences, and of becoming more and more complete as a human being. She achieved her goal of living in Cabora, she accepted her powers and tried to understand them, she learned about the role she could or could not have in history, she took risks, and she made a commitment. I think her life was a success, as a human being, and as an individual. The book ends with death, just as life does, but nevertheless there is something very heroic about Teresa, and I don't feel that she is a failure.

KG: Could she have achieved more if she had been born in the twentieth century?

BD: No, they would shut her up in an insane asylum, poor thing. Remember at the end of the book when they give electric shocks to the investigator? No, I think one of the great tragedies of our time is that the belief in magic has been lost. We are no longer astonished by natural things. We were astonished when men walked on the moon, but that was a long time ago, and we were astonished by the intelligent missiles used in Desert Storm; but day-to-day magic, the sense of the miracle of life, has been lost. And that's what Teresa represents, until she becomes integrated into a materialist society in the United States, and she begins to lose her magic. Why? Because she is in a society that no longer believes in magic, and magic needs to be recognized in order to exist. If Teresa showed up today and tried to do magic, do you think that anyone would notice? We have totally lost our capacity to perceive magic. We have to have a rational, logical interpretation for everything. If something happens that we don't understand, we call it charlatanry.

KG: Nevertheless, I think that outside Mexico City the people still believe in magic.

INTERVIEW

BD: Well, that depends on their social class, because you can go to Hermosillo and I'll bet that the middle and upper class there would not go to see Teresita today. But there are people from the small towns who still believe, like the thousands of people who made pilgrimages to the ranch in Querétaro, where the river water was said to cure cancer.

KG: Do you think that a return to the province (the area outside Mexico City) would be a way to rescue the magic?

BD: No, I think not. I think that we have to find another meaning for magic, and perhaps the vision of women can help because whether we like it or not, we are more connected to the earth, not biologically, but because we have been condemned to that connection, to being closer to the processes of life and death, and that sort of thing. And that is related to magic, too, because magic is the world of emotions, it is below or above cold reason, which for years now has not been working. [Reason] is no longer the absolute religion that it was fifty years ago; intuition is gaining ground, which pleases me immensely.

KG: What was the purpose of writing *Acechando al unicornio* (stalking the unicorn)?

BD: Pure malice. The theme of virginity is still taboo, and the interest in the topic continues to be morbid, so it was a challenge. Once I had compiled the book I discovered that it is an important contribution to the understanding of women in society. In the first place, it is a literary history; that is, you can see the transformation of literature through time. But what is more important is how it shows the changing attitudes toward feminine sexuality in different time periods. It is good to know where we are coming from in order to have a vision about where we want to go. In this sense, I'm not propagating sexist ideas; on the contrary, I am putting them in historical perspective so that they can be seen for what they are. Besides, literature itself tends to be critical. Even though the texts from the first half of the nineteenth century tend to accept the idea that a woman who has lost her virginity is stigmatized, by the later nineteenth century there begins to appear a more critical attitude and an attempt to change the concept of a fallen woman. So it is interesting to see this evolution, especially for the younger generations who have the idea that sexuality is very natural and they think that it's always been that way. A historical vision is like a lesson about where not to fall in the future.

KG: So that women will know how much they have progressed.

BD: Exactly! For example, I think that there is very little awareness in the generation of my daughter, who is twenty-five years old. They don't realize that the freedom which they take for granted is the result of a feminist struggle which began at least 150 years ago. That [struggle] is the focus of my next novel: the transformations that women have undergone throughout several generations as a result of the changes wrought by the feminist movement.

KG: Could you tell me more about this book?

BD: I would like to follow several generations of women, starting in about 1850 and arriving at about the year 2000. The title of the book will be *Quién recordará mi casa* (who will remember my house), and the focus is on women who have been totally marginal to the great events and movements of history. The great events will serve as a background for these marginal lives, these shut-in lives, and for this transformation which I perceive as a real growth in women, which has been more on a conscious level in recent generations. Nevertheless, in previous generations there already existed this impetus, this search, this need to find a greater meaning for our existence than being mothers and wives.

KG: What can you tell me about your book on Mexican women writers?

BD: I am putting together a series of essays about the development of Mexican literature written by women; it is a panoramic view.[6] In 1980 I detected a surge in women's writing in Mexico; it has continued throughout the eighties, and in the nineties it is really frenetic. I have been approaching

---

[6]*She is referring to* Mujer que publica, mujer pública, *mentioned in the introduction to part 4.*

INTERVIEW

this phenomenon from various different perspectives, such as the theme of sexuality in texts written by women, and their relation to literary movements, like modernism or postmodernism. And I always try to keep a sense of humor, because I believe that humor breaks with the rigid structures that we have been subjected to, and it allows in fresh air.

I was invited to participate in a panel discussion that was titled "What comes after postmodernism," and I thought, "What's this postmodernism hype?" Because we haven't been in on vanguardism, nor on modernism, and we weren't even invited to the banquet of romanticism. Women have always been on the periphery of all great literary movements; we haven't participated and we haven't been accepted. Many of us are now recovering at a rapid pace the earlier manifestations of the masculine literary tradition. We are integrating ourselves, but not in a strict way; we are combining genres, methods, different schools, different experiments. We are not confined within a particular school or "ism," but rather we are racing against time to create our own tradition, our own schools, which perhaps will influence masculine literature. I think that literature written by women is already influencing masculine literature. I couldn't swear to that, it's my intuition.

Therefore, I invented a term for this panel discussion; I said that women have always been in the "marginal post-neo-ism," that is, we are always behind and on the fringe of what is new. Women writers have always been tacked on to an existing literature, like pendants hanging there: "Look, here's a Rosario Castellanos[7] suddenly," and critics always try to fit us into a classification that is totally based on literature written by men. Movements are discovered after the fact of production. There is a period of time in which a certain type of literature is produced, and afterwards it is proclaimed romanticism. Then a woman who starts to write a generation later gets called a late romanticist, and she is stuck with that label. Therefore, if we separate the body of literature written by women and we begin to see it has a tradition of its own, we can get a better vision of

---

[7]See chapter 1, note 1, of this book.

what women are contributing to present-day literature. Otherwise, we will always be squeezed into a classification that doesn't fit us, like a foot forced into a shoe with a shoehorn.

I think that there already exists a body of literature written by Mexican women, an important corpus that deserves to be seen for itself, apart from literature written by men. But once we have a vision of a solid and multiple base of literature written by women, then Literature (with a capital *L*) is going to become the best that emerges from women's literature and the best that emerges from men's literature; it will all be integrated.

KG: In your collection of short stories, *Bestiario doméstico* (domestic bestiary), the protagonist of "Trilogía" (trilogy) seems to be a precursor of modern feminists. Is that your intention?

BD: Actually, Lilith [the protagonist] is projected as the mythification of the feminist with the possibility of being reintegrated into a couple. It entails a deconstruction of the patriarchal Christian myth for the purpose of constructing a new myth. Lilith is the woman who refuses to submit to Adam; she symbolizes the rebellious woman who loves her partner but not patriarchy. She doesn't want to be subjugated, but she is not a mankiller. She is growing, evolving, searching for herself, but she is always nostalgic for her companion, and she finally forms a new couple with the devil Sammael, who could also represent the darker side of man.

KG: Even though it is just a myth, your story could help women to understand where they come from, and to not feel alone. I noticed that many of Lilith's daughters committed suicide or became alcoholics. That is the high price that so many women pay for their liberation.

BD: Yes, the price is solitude and great pain. So many of my friends are alone; they have lost their partners because they are ahead of their time, and they are so different from what is considered normal. I consider myself very fortunate because even though my husband comes from a family in which the father was very macho, he rebelled against machismo. He went into psychoanalysis, he accepted his feminine side, he accepted

INTERVIEW

my masculine side, and we have tried to create a new way of being a couple. In that sense, Lilith is autobiographical.

KG: It is a great consolation to read works like yours, in which women take control of their own lives.

BD: That's what I want to do to an even greater degree in my next novel. I want to show that growth is achieved through pain, through rupture, through constant sacrifice. And I want to show the progress made through four or five generations of women. That's my concept now, but I get these crazy ideas and then I end up writing something totally different.

CHAPTER TWELVE

Magic and Play in
Brianda Domecq's
*La insólita historia
de la Santa de Cabora*
and *Once días . . . y algo más*

Although some use stories
as entertainment alone,
tales are, in their oldest sense,
a healing art.
Some are called to this healing art,
and the best, to my lights,
are those who have lain
with the story and found
all its matching parts
inside themselves and at depth.

C<small>LARISSA</small> P<small>INKOLA</small> E<small>STÉS</small>,
W<small>OMEN</small> W<small>HO</small> R<small>UN</small>
<small>WITH THE</small> W<small>OLVES</small>

F OLK HEALERS AND STORYTELLERS ARE ENGAGED IN SIMILAR AC-tivities: curing the spiritual maladies of our times. Thus, Brianda Domecq and her protagonist, the nineteenth-century *curandera* Teresa Urrea, have led analogous lives. Actually, their lives have intertwined across time and space, which makes both of their stories more powerful. But this power comes with a price, as Clarissa Pinkola Estés warns: "Absolutely, one is enabled in the story, in the medicine, by the amount of self that one is willing to sacrifice and put into it. . . . There must be a little spilled blood on every story if it is to carry the medicine" (464). Although Domecq devoted seventeen years of her life to Teresa's story, her secondary protagonist, an unnamed twentieth-century investigator, seems to have made an even greater sacrifice: the loss of her identity.

Domecq's novel, *La insólita historia de la Santa de Cabora* (the unusual story of the saint from Cabora), is divided into three parts. The first part has twenty sections that alternate between the investigator's story and that of Teresa Urrea, and a conclusion in which the two women both experience a fall and their stories seem to merge. The investigator has spent many years in the archives, researching Teresa's life, and she has decided to culminate her study by traveling to Teresa's home and interviewing some of her relatives. Her trip to Cabora is paralleled by the journey made by Teresa at the age of seven, from her native Sinaloa to the outskirts of Cabora. As the historian travels toward her destination, she remembers fragments of documents about Teresa: references to her in books, telegrams, political speeches, newspaper articles, and letters. These excerpts dance around in her head, tormenting her with their contradictory and often derogatory depiction of Teresa, and setting the stage for her obsessive search for the real Teresa, a human being rather than a myth. The historian leaves her briefcase—with all of the historical documents—

on the airplane, thus entering a new phase in which she identifies with Teresa rather than investigating her. Her obsession leads her up a steep hill and into the cave where Teresa once found the red dirt that she used for her miraculous cures. The investigator's guide abandons her there, and she runs down the hill in a panic, falling into Teresa's life.

Meanwhile, Teresa is growing up near Cabora, in an extremely poor family of ranch hands. With the help of an old woman, she manages to learn how to read and write, and she sends her rich landowner father, Tomás Urrea, a letter. He impulsively decides to recognize his illegitimate daughter, and he accepts Teresa into his home. With only a few glitches, she adjusts to her new status, and everything is going well until she falls from her horse. At this point, Domecq's two protagonists merge into one, and that one is Teresa. Part 2 of the novel tells about Teresa's miraculous cures and her increasing fame as a saint and a healer, and part 3 describes Teresa's life in exile in the United States, where she is ordered to live because her message of social reform threatens the dictatorship of Porfirio Díaz. The novel's epilogue has the investigator waking up in the twentieth century after having been in a coma for three months, believing that she is Teresa Urrea. The doctors take her to an insane asylum and administer electric shocks.

Like Silvia Molina's novels, this text is metafictional, because it is a story about the investigation of a story. However, *La insólita historia de la Santa de Cabora* shows the investigatory process evolving into a living experience, rather than a writing experience. The act of writing is suppressed. The narrator is unidentified and unobtrusive, with no epic situation and no self-conscious reference to the writing process. Even though this is obviously a literary game that Domecq is playing, the blurring of the distinction between writing and living, or rewriting and reliving, has interesting implications. Susan Rubin Suleiman, referring to the emancipatory potential of feminist intertextuality, has affirmed:

> Extrapolating a bit, we arrive at the contemporary—and contemporary feminist—insight that the stories we tell about reality *construe* the real, rather than merely reflect it. Whence the possibility or the hope, that through the rewriting of

old stories and the invention of new forms of language
for doing so, it is the world as well as words that will be
transformed. (143)

There are many feminist messages imbedded in this text, imparted by example, not by rhetoric, and which have the potential to "construe the real." Woman-to-woman bonds based on friendship and the sharing of knowledge illustrate the power of female solidarity. Teresa's rebellion against the restrictive roles of women is living proof that everything is possible if you put your mind to it. But there is an even deeper message, and that is the need to rescue the instinctual, intuitive, imaginative powers that women have, which Estés has identified with the female archetype of the Wild Woman, as she explains her term:

> So, the word *wild* here is not used in its modern pejorative
> sense, meaning out of control, but in its original sense, which
> means to live a natural life, one in which the *criatura,* creature,
> has innate integrity and healthy boundaries. These words, *wild*
> and *woman,* cause women to remember who they are and what
> they are about. They create a metaphor to describe the force
> which funds all females. They personify a force that women
> cannot live without. (8)

As patroness of all painters, writers, sculptors, dancers, thinkers, prayer makers, and seekers, the Wild Woman is the inspiration for invention. She also is a healer, for she carries the medicine for all things. "She carries stories and dreams and words and songs and signs and symbols. She is both vehicle and destination" (Estés 12). The Wild Woman, then, is the key to understanding Teresa's curative powers and Domecq's narrative powers. It is significant that after their fall, both Teresa and the investigator remain in a coma for three months, and when they come out of it, they are in a trance. Teresa heals while in this trance; the investigator assumes Teresa's identity and tells her story while in this state. The investigator's trance is an exaggeration of Domecq's obsessive condition as she wrote her novel. Estés explains this kind of narrative:

One of the oldest ways of telling, which intrigues me greatly, is the passionate trance state, wherein the teller "senses" the audience—be it an audience of one or of many—and then enters a state in the world between worlds, where a story is "attracted" to the trance-teller and told through her. This is the storyteller furthering soul-making. (19)

Domecq has also "sensed" her audience, which is why she has written her story as a novel, as fiction, so that she can play with these ideas, explore their potential, and not be taken away for electric shocks. Just to be certain that everyone realizes that she is playing, she has included a quote by the Argentinean writer Jorge Luis Borges—a man famous for his literary play—as the epigraph to her novel: "The agnostic is an individual who doesn't believe in the certainty of knowledge, but who can play with the possibilities and weave hypotheses that may be enchanting or terrible" (5).[1]

After the epigraph, Domecq includes a playful introit, or introductory prayer, in which Santa Teresa arrives in Heaven and requests admission. God rejects her because she isn't registered, and then demands to know her genealogy, so Teresa produces a long list of women identified only by their first name. The reader is not informed as to whether or not God accepts this nontraditional genealogy, but one reviewer hypothesized that Teresa was not allowed into heaven, so she had to come back to earth as the investigator.[2]

The intriguing connections, overlappings, and blurring of the boundaries between Domecq, the investigator, and Teresa are reminiscent of a phenomenon Susan Rubin Suleiman has called "playing with the boundaries of the self," which she identifies as a necessary part of artistic creativity:

> Playing, as Freud and Winnicott (among others) have shown us, is the activity through which the human subject most freely

---

[1] *All quotes in this chapter, unless otherwise identified, are from* La insólita historia de la Santa de Cabora *(Mexico City: Planeta, 1990). All translations are mine.*
[2] *See Mirta A. González in the Works Cited.*

MAGIC AND PLAY

and inventively constitutes herself or himself. To play is to affirm an "I," an autonomous subjectivity that exercises control over a world of possibilities; at the same time, and contrarily, it is in playing that the "I" can experience itself in its most fluid and boundaryless state. Barthes speaks of being "liberated from the binary prison, putting oneself in a state of infinite expansion."[3] Winnicott calls the play experience "one of a nonpurposive state, as one might say a sort of ticking over of the unintegrated personality" —and adds a few pages later that "it is only here, in this unintegrated state of the personality, that that which we describe as creative can appear." (Suleiman 179)[4]

Playing with the boundaries of the self can create ruptured and fragmented images that elude restrictive classifications, just as some twentieth-century narratives by women deliberately fracture traditional sequence in order to evade the closure imposed by traditional plots.[5] Fragmentation can be seen as something creative, then, something that provides a fertile multiplicity of identities. Through writing, an author is able to reinvent herself over and over again, which Domecq identifies as one of the tasks of the woman writer:

> A woman writes to reinvent herself, to discover herself, to define herself. Words become instruments to delve into the flesh, into reality, into the subconscious, as a way of finding one's own identity. Words can break clichés, demythify, subdue the false metaphors, and demasculinize the image of woman. (February 1981, 3)

Fragmentation of the self, then, is seen as something positive in this novel. In contrast, there is another kind of fragmentation, that of narrative, which is used as a deconstruction tool by the author. When Teresa doubts her revolutionary mission, for example, she remembers the rhetoric that her mentor Lauro Aguirre employed to encourage her to join the struggle. She realizes that

---

[3] *Barthes*, Roland Barthes par lui-meme, *137.*
[4] *D.D. Winnicott,* Playing and Reality *(New York: Basic, 1971), 55, 64.*
[5] *See Duplessis's* Writing Beyond the Ending, *15.*

the revolutionary rhetoric—like the dictator's speeches—can be broken down into insignificant pieces: "Words, they were just words and like [the folk healer] Huila had taught her, with words we fragment existence: everything becomes little pieces of the truth, interchangeable and relative" (339). In part 1 of the novel, the author uses fragmentation to refute the official rhetoric by utilizing an intense discourse/counter-discourse technique in which the "code-switching" takes place within paragraphs and even within sentences.[6] The narrator's voice reveals the investigator's thoughts and is presented in normal type. Other voices are presented in italics, including representations of the official story (political speeches, news releases, or official history) and a multitude of other voices that represent the conflicting views of Teresa proffered by news writers and ordinary people. Because all of these voices are presented in italics and separated only by suspension points, the words themselves must reveal the speaker's identity, or at least his/her attitude:

> *The miraculous apparition of the young Teresa Urrea in the ranch of Cabora is a confirmed fact . . . Was Teresa an apparition? . . . Miss Urrea, in full knowledge and malice, planned and led uprisings against the legitimate government . . . the Tomóchic uprising is explained by the robbery perpetrated against the people by the Governor of the State, Sir Lauro Carrillo, who took from the church of Tomóchic a valuable painting that he planned to give to Carmelita Díaz . . .*
>   *The Saint visits God when she wishes, she speaks familiarly with Saint Peter and she corresponds regularly with the Holy Spirit . . .* and with her, too; if not, she wouldn't go to Cabora . . . (44)

These fragments reveal the popular view of Teresa as a saint, the government's view of Teresa as a subversive element, and an explanation offered for the Tomóchic uprising, from the townspeople's point of view. This same counterdiscursive technique is employed many times in the first part of the novel, as the narrator interjects an ironic comment into an official explanation, or presents an opposing point of view.

---

[6]Code-switching *is a linguistic term that usually refers to changing languages in midsentence. Domecq is switching speakers rather than languages.*

MAGIC AND PLAY

Fragmentation also reveals the investigator's confusion and torment:

> She closed her eyes: the answer was there, silently waiting for her: she was crazy, totally crazy. *Teresa Urrea belongs in body to psychopathy and in spirit to the disciples of Allan Kardec* . . . To think that she had been "chosen", that her steps were guided by the will of one called Teresita, that information reached her by divine (?) order, *with these weapons, the so-called "saint" would not have surpassed acute neurasthenia if it had not been for the fanaticism of the masses* . . . so that she could fulfill an unknown mission! Crazy! *The moral and intellectual qualities of the young woman were in marked contrast to the vice and ignorance of the social environment in which she was raised* . . . Where was the "saint" when she forgot her briefcase? What "mission" was she going to fulfill with empty hands? (69)

The solution to the narrator's confusion, doubts, and inability to take her research further is the supernatural fusion of her spirit with that of Teresa. The reader's willing suspension of disbelief is encouraged by the foreshadowing of this event by means of a series of dreams in which the investigator falls into a different reality. The world of dreams, an important element in Estés' Wild Woman archetype, thus prefigures the historian's merger with Teresa.

What we are really dealing with here is magic. Magic is an important theme throughout the novel: black magic, healing magic, religious magic (miracles), reincarnation, extrasensory perception, mental telepathy, prophecy, and mysterious connections between people and events. Domecq's narrative techniques blend elements of magic realism,[7] *lo real maravilloso* (the marvelous real),[8] and social realism (in which there is a sociopolitical

---

[7]*Magic realism is a literary style (rather than movement) that combines a detailed account of common, everyday events with a few supernatural touches. Gabriel García Márquez's* One Hundred Years of Solitude *is a classic example, but Elena Garro's* Recollections of Things to Come *is also noteworthy.*

[8]*Lo real maravilloso is another literary trend in which natural phenomena are presented as marvelous. People stand in awe of nature's great wonders, such as volcanoes or jungles. A good example is Alejo Carpentier's* The Lost Steps.

message). Magic is central to this text because of the fusion of the two protagonists—which makes a statement about the relationship between a storyteller and her story—and because of Teresa's struggle to understand her powers, which becomes a search for identity and purpose. Teresa's struggle for comprehension is repeated by the investigator and by Domecq, and thus the novel becomes a Chinese box of inquiry within, or by means of, another inquiry.

Teresa's magical cures may be seen as the power of suggestion or of hypnotism, combined with an extensive knowledge of the healing qualities of plants and herbs. But there is something more than that, something that drew the investigator to Teresa's story, because Teresa is somehow special. She embodies the powerful elements of the archetypal Wild Woman: intuition, imagination, connection to the earth, creativity, and playfulness. Her magic is opposed by the political power and violence perpetrated by the dictator Porfirio Díaz, and by the threat of oblivion. The investigator sees the conflict between Díaz and Teresa as a war between good and evil, a mythical battle in which tyranny had triumphed when Teresa was sent into exile. But Teresa had minor triumphs before her defeat, like the time when a man sent by Díaz to assassinate her fell to his knees and begged forgiveness, and the preliminary victory of the people of Tomóchic, before they were all massacred. In both cases, her telepathic powers forewarned her of danger. And even though her exile did precipitate Teresa's fall into oblivion, the investigator appeared one hundred years later to rescue her from obscurity.

Teresa's magic is also seen in relation to science, though not necessarily in opposition to scientific knowledge. Rather, her powers are presented as something that science has not yet recognized. For example, when Teresa dies for the first time, she is actually in a coma, but the doctor diagnoses her as dead. He doesn't recognize the life and power that lie dormant within her. The folk healer Huila is the only one that realizes that Teresa is not really dead. Teresa's "resurrection" is seen as a miracle, and don Tomás (Teresa's father) dismisses the doctor as a quack.

There are many explanations offered for Teresa's miraculous cures and visionary powers: she is an agent of God or of the

MAGIC AND PLAY

devil, she suffers from epilepsy or hysteria, she is a witch, a saint, or a fraud. (There is a humorous echo here of all of the contradictory physical descriptions of Teresa: tall/short, heavy/slender, old/young for her age, blond/brunette/redhead, etc.) Teresa's political mentor, Lauro Aguirre, has a pseudoscientific interpretation of her powers:

> It all has a perfectly scientific explanation, my beloved Tomás, even though you with your stubborn rationalism don't want to accept it. Spontaneous somnambulism, preceded by a mystical cataleptic attack; possession by an astral body; possibly contact with other dimensions. She'll get over it with time. A simple phenomenon of magnetism and electricity that we still haven't mastered, but scientific, my friend, one hundred per cent scientific, I assure you. (168)

Although the narrator is obviously making fun of Lauro's interpretation, the idea that some scientific explanation may be discovered in the future is not totally dismissed. In her last place of residence, Clifton, Arizona, Teresa befriends the local doctor, and they manage to cooperate in order to cure the illnesses of many of the townspeople. They also cooperate on the fund raising for and the construction of the town's only hospital. Teresa and the doctor believe that they can learn from each other, and perhaps find some logical explanation for Teresa's healing powers.

If there is an explanation for Teresa's magic, it probably can not be expressed in words, according to Teresa's own insight, which probably eliminates the possibility of that explanation being logical. Teresa, following Huila's teaching, saw language as something that obscures reality, not something that illuminates it. Returning to the concept of words as fragments of reality, the act of naming something is seen as an act of separating that thing from the rest of reality. Teresa concludes:

> Understanding that did not mean being able to repeat it with words but rather being able to see it: it was the secret of healing, the secret of life and death. She learned to look behind the names of things, to look for the threads that connected them to the rest of life, to discover hidden meanings in order to

> turn around the intellect, to elude reason, to liberate herself
> from language and to see that indivisible flow that was,
> according to the teacher, the true reality. (133–34)

Paradoxically, Domecq is attempting to express with words what cannot be expressed with words. She can only hint at the ineffable quality of magic, life, and death. She depends on the reader to follow the dotted line, to feel what cannot be said, to intuit what cannot be reasoned, just as Teresa depended on the people's belief in her powers in order to cure them. Domecq invites the reader's cooperation for the purpose of "construing the real," in order to have an effect on the world.

Returning to some of the concepts presented in the preceding chapters, many of them can be productively applied to this text as well. Intertextuality is of course essential to the discourse/counter-discourse technique undermining the government's official version of history. In Domecq's novel, this technique relies upon an alternative narrative structure consisting of rapid-fire code-switching among multiple narrators. Although counter-discourse is predominant in part 1, parts 2 and 3 present a more positive, alternative discourse, a different way of seeing Teresa and of telling her story. The different way of seeing is metaphorically presented as a fusion of the investigator with Teresa; thus, she is seen from within. The result is a different way of telling her story, because the investigator experiences Teresa's life, including her thoughts, emotions, and bodily functions, which are described in very unsaintly ways.

The inclusion of Teresa's body in the text—the description of physical changes undergone in puberty and adolescence, her physical desires, her maternity—is a marked deviation from traditional hagiography, in which the body is seen simply as a vessel for the spirit. The revaluation of the female body is another characteristic of the Wild Woman archetype, as Estés explains:

> The idea in our culture of body solely as sculpture is wrong.
> Body is not marble. That is not its purpose. Its purpose is to
> protect, contain, support, and fire the spirit and soul within it,
> to be a repository for memory, to fill us with feeling—that is

MAGIC AND PLAY

> the supreme psychic nourishment. It is to lift us and propel us, to fill us with feeling to prove that we exist, that we are here, to give us grounding, heft, weight. It is wrong to think of it as a place we leave in order to soar to the spirit. The body is the launcher of those experiences. (206)

Teresa is portrayed in this novel as a human being, not as a saint or a witch, but just a person with a special connection to the forces of life and death, a connection that everyone can feel, to one degree or another. She utilizes all of the information available to her, including the teachings of Huila, messages encoded in dreams, inexplicable visions, and the knowledge provided by her own body.

Domecq has managed to tell "the other side of the story" even though some of that other side is ineffable. She has also "written beyond the ending," because Teresa does not limit herself to marriage and children; she searches for something more, and in that end she has formed nontraditional alliances with other women and with some of the men in her life, particularly with the doctor from Clifton. By placing Teresa in the center of her narrative, Domecq has rescued a character condemned to the periphery in Porfirio Díaz's time and to oblivion in our time. As she explores the narrative possibilities of magic and play, the author manages to bring her protagonist back to life.

Magic and play also are important elements in Domecq's first novel based on her own kidnapping, although in the earlier work they are survival tactics rather than resurrection techniques. Subjected to the extreme pressures and uncertainties of her kidnapping, Leo, the protagonist of *Once días . . . y algo más* (eleven days . . . and even more), instinctively resorts to the strengths of the Wild Woman archetype in order to stay alive. Intuition, imagination, creativity, playfulness, and belief in everyday miracles all help Leo to survive.

Separated from everybody she loves and everything that she owns, and cut off from the visual world by adhesive tape over her eyes, the protagonist is forced to engage in constant self-examination. Her introspection results in her playing with the boundaries of her self: her character splits, and one side observes and criticizes the other. This split begins at the moment of her kidnapping, when two armed men are forcing her to move out of the driver's seat of her car:

> "I'm moving, I'm moving," my voice comes out with a squeak that opens the first crack of light in my trembling mass of fear. My consciousness begins to fracture. A small, cold and ironic voice orders me to get control of myself, while I sink into deeper and deeper desperation. I have to calm down, I think. (9)[9]

This little voice accompanies Leo throughout her ordeal, sometimes criticizing her, but often forcing her to think things through, to put things in order and to take stock of the situation. The voice is strongest at the two points of rupture: at the beginning and at the end of her kidnapping. The division seems a protective device, as she distances herself from the source of her emotional upheaval. During the climactic and chaotic scene at the police station (after her rescue), Leo is spiritually absent:

> Laughter, hugs, questions . . . but I am quiet, with ice in my veins. Something that wanted to be an emotion died before it happened. I was empty of all reaction or feeling and I thought I was slipping away from myself (as if I were living and observing everything from an immense distance), while my body hugged my mother, my brother, my father, and my voice asked how he felt. (232)

Fragmentation of the self in this case helps the protagonist to avoid emotional overload. In contrast, the narrative is not fragmented as it is in *La insólita historia de la Santa de Cabora*. Rather, the narrative is carefully knit together, with an obviously chronological structure and a consistent, first-person narrator. Everything is meticulously ordered—with only slight variation, there is one chapter for each day of captivity—as if this external order imposed upon the experience could somehow get all of the cha-

---

[9] *All quotes in this section, unless otherwise identified, are from* Once días . . . y algo más *(Mexico City: HARLA, 1991). All translations are mine.*

otic and contradictory emotions under control. The only time that the narrative is fragmented is when the Boss of the kidnappers is speaking to Leo. Her thoughts interrupt his obnoxious speeches about words of honor and respecting the terms of the agreement, undermining his authority:

> "The negotiations are going quite well. Your husband and your father have comprehended the seriousness of the matter, the necessity to comply with what has been stipulated. I already told you. I am a man of his word. I will keep my promises . . ."
> *"My God! The broken record. Truly, if it is a battle of personalities, I am going to win; at least I don't repeat the same story twice to the same kidnapper."*
> ". . . and I will bring you daily news. But right now I can't stay here and chat with you like I would prefer, because we have a little matter to attend to . . ." (95)[10]

The interruption of the Boss's words by Leo's ironic thoughts is a precursor of the discourse/counter-discourse technique that Domecq has developed much further in her second novel.

In addition to playing with the boundaries of her self, the protagonist of *Once días . . . y algo más* also plays with the boundaries—and with the identities—of her captors. In the beginning, the boundaries were obvious: there was a marked barrier between the kidnappers and their victim. But Leo instinctively begins to cross that barrier and to melt the boundaries by discovering the natural human connections between them. Later, she recognizes the purpose of her own game, and she pursues it deliberately:

> [The kidnapper] would like to ignore me, but like a moth around a lightbulb, he can't distance himself for very long. He doesn't understand my game. Instead of scorn and rejection, acceptance and admiration; in stead of rage and resistance, accommodation and jokes. I feel his confusion. He knows that I am playing, but he has doubts, because this isn't the game he expected. (116)

---

[10]*For the sake of clarity, I have put Leo's thoughts in italics*

Leo makes up funny names for her captors: Santa Claus, the Bartender, the Rascal, and the Snoop. She plays word games, dominos, and *la Gallinita Ciega* (somewhat like blind man's bluff) with the kidnappers. They tell jokes, exchange recipes, listen to music, listen to each other's stories, and give each other advice. The games are fun, but they are also serious, at least for Leo. She realizes that inside their reduced world, there are subtleties of human relations that have been forgotten on the outside. By telling these men her life's story, she begins to rediscover her own identity and to see herself from a new perspective. She also is installing herself in their psyches, establishing herself as a person, not a victim, and plotting her revenge: "No, they will not be able to forget me, perhaps that is my revenge . . . when in future nights of insomnia I will occupy their thoughts again, and they will miss me" (199).

The game is dangerous because Leo doesn't control the rules. She often does not know what the rules are, because they are sometimes set by the Boss but often broken by everybody else. She is also aware of the danger to her own psyche, as she becomes more and more involved with her captors. There is one electric moment when she is physically attracted by the Rascal, but she backs away and averts sure disaster. As Domecq has explained, these bonds are a natural human reaction to a situation of extreme dependency, and their severance was exceedingly painful. The recuperation process was aided by the writing of her novel, which is another example of the healing qualities of narrative.

Domecq's belief in everyday magic is evident, because she presents both the formation of human bonds and the recovery from their rupture as miraculous. However, while still a captive, Leo is concerned that she will not be understood by the outside world:

> In this world in which life is always on the line one cannot avoid the creation of bonds, the mutual commitment, the establishment of an affection like that which grows between companions of war, both profound and distressing. I'm not trying to justify it or even explain it. It's like discovering a perfect metaphor in the middle of a dreadful poem. It is one of the little miracles of life, ephemeral and inexplicable, in

MAGIC AND PLAY

which you have to believe in order for them to happen, and who out there still believes in miracles? Who is going to believe me when I tell them that I made friends and that thanks to them the days went by more quickly, the experience acquired meaning, and nothing was as terrible as it might have seemed? (205)

Leo believes that it will take a miracle for someone to believe and understand her. Being agnostic, she does not use the word *miracle* in a religious sense, but in the sense of secular magic, something extraordinary. Something wondrous does happen, and that is her husband's comprehension of those unusual bonds, because he felt something similar in his relationship over the telephone with the Boss. Leo concludes: "I could finally cry, with my mouth open in astonishment; I understood: [my husband] Ariel was the miracle" (235).

Once días...y algo más is a nonfictional novel, a documentary in novelized form, about a serious and potentially devastating crime, told from the victim's point of view. Such material does not lend itself to the themes of magic and play, and yet they are both important elements in the text and the basis for the author/protagonist's survival and recovery. This novel is another example of alternative discourse because it presents a different way of seeing, a different way of experiencing—and surviving—an extremely threatening situation. It also makes a powerful statement about the potential connections between human beings that transcend all social and economic differences. Published eleven years before the more sophisticated and complex novel, *La insólita historia de la Santa de Cabora*, it nevertheless contains all of the elements that are so masterfully developed in the later work.

CONCLUSION

THE FOUR AUTHORS PRESENTED IN THIS BOOK HAVE BROKEN their window bars and discovered a new vision of themselves and of Mexican society. They have all learned to see beyond the artificial constraints put upon them by an archaic patriarchal system. Each one has her own reasons for writing. Elena Poniatowska says she writes to belong—to a country and to its people—and to give voice to the voiceless. Her strong identification with her interviewees makes their stories come alive, promoting solidarity and a heightened awareness of the need for social and political reform in Mexico. Angeles Mastretta also mentions giving a voice to those who cannot tell their own story, those who are marginalized by society and history, and then she confesses, "I write to be alive." For her, writing is a passion, a source of pleasure, love, laughter, companionship, and doubt. Silvia Molina writes to reinvent herself, to be—at least in fiction—the woman that she aspires to be in reality. Thus she creates positive role models for herself and for her readers. Brianda Domecq writes because she has to; she was born to write. Kidnapped by her first novel and possessed by her second, this author invests such vitality and urgency in her writing that the narrative pulsates with life.

All of these women are feminists, but not militants. They all have been married, with children. They write to criticize machismo and to present strong women as protagonists in the drama of Mexican life. The Mexican macho is always ready to squash a woman, according to Elena Poniatowska, but in her writing she shows women who refused to be squashed. Besides utilizing resilient female characters in her fictional works—notably Jesusa Palancares in *Hasta no verte, Jesús mío* (here's to you, Jesus)—Poniatowska has portrayed the strength and solidarity of the Mexican women in her testimonial works. In *Massacre in Mexico* she reveals the sorrow and fortitude of the mothers who mourn

CONCLUSION

the death of their children, as well as the energy and spunk of the young women such as Tita and Nacha, who served as organizers and leaders of the student protests. *Nada, nadie* (nothing, nobody) also immortalizes the mourning women, and sings the praises of the women who volunteered to help others and the seamstresses who organized to fight for better working conditions.

Angeles Mastretta laments her feelings of guilt and responsibility that tie her to the house and her children, and she resents her husband's ability to shut out the world while he works. Yet she is optimistic about the possibilities for her daughter, as she observes the rapid advances being made by the latest generation of Mexican women. In *Mexican Bolero,* Mastretta skillfully denounces the patriarchal patterns in the Mexican family and politics, and in *Mujeres de ojos grandes* (women with big eyes) she extols the creativity and strength of ordinary women who react in unusual ways to difficult situations.

Both Silvia Molina and Brianda Domecq have chosen supportive males and nontraditional roles for themselves in real life, whereas in their writing they criticize nonsupportive males and the restrictive roles that are often imposed upon Mexican women. Molina has created one of the best examples of a positive female role model in her novel *La familia vino del norte* (the family came from the north), and in *Imagen de Héctor* (image of Hector) she shows how to demystify the past in order to remake the present and shape one's future. Domecq has portrayed a consummate survivor in *Once días . . . y algo más* (eleven days . . . and even more). The protagonist of this novel is not entirely passive—although passivity is one of her survival strategies—because she reaches out to her captors, establishing ties with them and affirming her identity as a person. In Domecq's second novel, Teresa is successful in her own way, escaping an extremely oppressive situation and forging her own destiny.

What all of these women contribute to literature is an internal view of women's experience. Women can present events from a different perspective, which Domecq calls tangential and other theorists have called marginal or peripheral. According to Molina, by sharing the interior reality of females, literature can help

CONCLUSION

women to know themselves better. These writers are experimenting with alternative narrative structures that can better convey their messages, and such innovations will probably have an effect on literature produced by men as well.

The work of all four of these authors has a significant intertextual relationship with the public record, which is explicit in Poniatowka's, Molina's, and Domecq's books, and implicit in Mastretta's novel. Intertextuality is a transformational process in which the meaning of the original text may be either subverted or amplified. Excerpts from the official discourse energize these authors' texts, providing a backboard from which the new meaning can rebound; thus, they finance their own subversion, helping to create a dialogue in the same space where a monologue once reigned. All of these authors refer to the official story directly or indirectly, then provide eyewitness accounts and a multitude of other sources that contradict that public record and present another side of the story.

In the case of supportive intertextuality, the excerpts offer analogous situations in different times and places, or different perspectives on the same subject. Therefore, they enhance the universality of the text and augment the productive multiplicity of meanings. This supportive process is particularly evident in *Massacre in Mexico* and *Nada, nadie,* because Poniatowska uses excerpts from the same Nahuatl poems in both texts, establishing links between catastrophes that occurred in 1521, 1968, and 1985.

Mastretta's *Mexican Bolero,* told from the point of view of a politician's wife, only alludes to the official account of the governor's life as presented by newspapers and history books, without ever quoting these sources. The intertextual relationship with these sources is implied, however, by the narrator's reference to fictional news stories and speeches that have obvious, real-life counterparts. In this novel, intertextuality is subversive, because the narrator blatantly contradicts the content of the original sources.

In *La familia vino del norte,* Molina creates an intertextual relationship between her novel and many other texts, some of which are within her fictional space and others that are exterior to her text. Internally, Molina uses excerpts from Manuel's article, the

CONCLUSION

grandfather's diary, and Manuel's and Dorotea's letters. She also refers to several external texts: history books, a historical novel, a play about the revolution, a novel by Jean Rhys, and a short story by Boris Pilnyak. All of these original works are transformed in Molina's novel, because she uses them to forge her own narrative. In *Imagen de Héctor* (image of Héctor), Molina presents a multitude of descriptions and assessments of her father, from which she chooses the elements she judges to be true, in order to compile her own montage.

Domecq uses fragmentation of the official discourse as a deconstruction tool, chopping the public documents about Teresa Urrea into little pieces, then presenting these segments, interspersed with contradictory evidence and ironic commentary. She also uses fragmentation to present multiple perspectives of Teresa, creating a new whole.

Intertextuality is thus an important element in both counter- and alternative discourse. Poniatowska's counter-discourse tells the victim's side of the story, presenting an ironic contrast between what government officials said and what they did. Her alternative discourse is more positive and life-affirming, because it presents the courage, fortitude, and love of the Mexican people. Mastretta's counter-discourse, like Poniatowska's, constitutes the unmasking of corrupt government officials, drawing its power from a similar contrast between official words and deeds. Her alternative discourse is the telling of a woman's own story, from her marginalized position within Mexican society. The authority of this version of events is enhanced by the author's fidelity to the time period and the credibility of the narrator. In order to tell her side of the story, the narrator has appropriated masculine discourse and transformed the traditional romance plot into a story that ends "happily ever after" because of her husband's death. Duplicity is another important element of Mastretta's alternative discourse, because she relies on literary cosmetics to soften the hard edges of the reality she is criticizing. The author's own persona is safely covered up with a playful yet dramatic mask.

Molina uses temporal leapfrog, imbedded texts, and intertextuality to create an alternative narrative structure for her novels. An alternative ideology is presented by telling the other side

CONCLUSION

of the story and presenting multiple perspectives, none of which is privileged as the truth. Molina writes beyond the ending by creating new choices for female protagonists, and by using her narrative to reparent herself. All of these strategies create an alternative discourse that, rather than being counterdiscursive, only modifies the official discourse. Molina does not wish to eliminate the official history of her family and country, but she tries to make it more truthful, creating a more human image of her father, her other family members, and herself.

Domecq creates counter-discourse when she contradicts the official history of Teresa Urrea, and when she interrupts the Boss in *Once días . . . y algo más*. She generates alternative discourse in both novels when she presents a different way of seeing, and of telling, a story. She is so involved in her story that she pulls the reader in with her, creating what verges on being a living experience rather than a literary experience. She invites the reader into Teresa's life, and into Leo's ordeal. To do this she invokes the powers of the Wild Woman archetype: intuition, imagination, belief in magic, play, dreams, and a revaluation of the body. By means of humor, games, and an exaltation of essential human values, Domecq plays with the boundaries between her self, her characters, and her readers. Her writing is a powerful example of the healing qualities of literature: she cures Teresa of oblivion, she assuages her own obsessions, she searches for her own identity and a meaning to life, and with her first novel she helps her own family understand the emotions and complexities of her ordeal.

All four of these writers have played with and expanded upon the diverse powers of literature. Poniatowska reveals the power of narrative to promote social and political awareness. Mastretta extols literature as entertainment, and yet underneath that diversion lies an important social message. Molina offers literature as self-empowerment, because she transforms the writing of her family and historians, making herself an author of events, rather than a secondary character or narrator. She also uses literature as personal therapy, and to advance the struggle toward self-realization. Literature can be a means to humanize mythic figures, such as Molina's father and Domecq's protagonist, Teresa Urrea. It

CONCLUSION

also may humanize figures that have been traditionally scorned or presented as one-sided, such as the kidnappers in Domecq's first novel.

In the past fifteen years, these authors have significantly enhanced the image of women in Mexican narrative, providing alternatives to the old MalincheGuadalupe quandary and enlivening the images inscribed on Mexican women's imagination. Social and economic conditions are changing for Mexican women; increasing numbers of females are becoming doctors, lawyers, writers, professors, and even academic deans and directors of schools. It is fitting that literature not only reflect this developing reality but also encourage it, amplify it, and hasten its pace by making women aware of their escalating possibilities. For those women who have already attained autonomy, it is encouraging and energizing to see their struggles and successes recorded and legitimized in writing.

In the next ten years, Mexican women will be producing many new narratives that will expand upon the themes presented here. Poniatowska's novel about the astronomer will address Mexico's conflictive relationship with technology, and if the scientist's wife plays an important role, she may deal with the issues of a two-profession couple. Her forthcoming novel about a North American woman in Mexico will deal with some sensitive cross-cultural issues that are being confronted daily in the United States, in our interior and foreign policies and—on a personal level—in our homes, schools, and businesses. Mastretta's future novel about a woman who works in a pharmacy and believes in the powers of folk healers may further Domecq's discussion of the interplay between science and magic. Mastretta's projected work about her father may expand upon Molina's personal and historical research and further the possibilities of literary reparenting.

Molina's novel about a woman receiving anonymous letters from her estranged husband could turn into a proclamation of independence or a reworking of the love relationship in a modern couple. Domecq's panoramic essay on Mexican women writers will help place these and other narratives in their historical context and offer new perspectives on literature. Her novel about four or five generations of women may reflect the history of

CONCLUSION

women's liberation in the United States and Mexico and its effects on women in the late twentieth century.[1]

In the future, thanks to these and other pioneering authors, Mexican women will not have to fight so hard for the right to be trained as writers, to have time to write, and to get their books published. They will not have to deal with the image of the female writer as a rare bird, an oddity to be tolerated with amusement. New paths through the literary jungle have been beaten down. It will be easier for those who follow.

The four authors presented in this book can also show us the importance of "lying with a story," in order to find all the matching parts within ourselves.[2] In each of these remarkable women the reader may find a part of himself or herself, or a part that he/she wishes to develop. Thus, reading their works can be an act of self-discovery, as it has been for me. In Elena Poniatowska I have discovered inner beauty, and the courage to protest injustice. Angeles Mastretta's energy, humor, and drama bring out my love of life and of play-acting: the part of me that comes alive when I perform, whether I'm teaching, dancing, or playing with my children. Silvia Molina's shyness and reserve represent the side of me that I must conquer each time that I walk into a classroom or a conference hall, but this side is productive, contemplative, and self-sufficient. Brianda Domecq has had to straddle two cultures, as I have, and her successful accommodation to both worlds has enriched her writing and her life. She reminds me of the importance of humor, of everyday miracles, of essential human values, and of the infinite connections between people, places, and events.

I have found four friends, four teachers, four inspirations. I offer them to you, the reader, in the knowledge that upon perusing their works, each one of you will find something more: something challenging and meaningful to you.

---

[1] *Other writers will be making significant contributions, also. In addition to those referred to in the introduction to this book, I would like to mention the following authors, who are in varying stages of their careers: María Luisa Puga, Luisa Josefina Hernández, Carmen Boullosa, Aline Petterson, Laura Esquivel, Sabina Berman, Margo Glantz, Bárbara Jacobs, Teresa Aveleyra Sadowska, and Cristina Pacheco.*

[2] *This is Clarissa Pinkola Estés' expression, presented in the epigraph of chapter 12 of this book.*

WORKS CITED

INTRODUCTION

Gilbert, Sandra and Susan Gubar. *The Mad Woman in the Attic: The Woman Writer and the Nineteenth-century literary imagination.* New Haven: Yale UP, 1979.

Gold, Janet. "Feminine Space and the Discourse of Silence: Yolanda Oreamuno, Elena Poniatowska, and Luisa Valenzuela." *In the Feminine Mode.* Ed. Noel Valis and Carol Maier. Cranbury, NJ: Associated UP, 1990. 195–203.

Heilbrun, Carolyn. *Writing a Woman's Life.* New York: W. W. Norton, 1988.

Jenny, Laurent. "The Strategy of Form." *French Literary Theory Today.* Ed. Tzvetan Todorov. Cambridge: Cambridge UP, 1982.

Terdiman, Richard. *Discourse/Counter-Discourse.* Ithaca: Cornell UP, 1985.

PART ONE: ELENA PONIATOWSKA

Barry, Tom, ed. *Mexico: A Country Guide.* Albuquerque: Inter-Hemispheric Education Resource Center, 1992.

Jenny, Laurent. "The Strategy of Form." *French Literary Theory Today.* Ed. Tzvetan Todorov. Cambridge: Cambridge UP, 1982.

León-Portilla, Miguel. *La visión de los vencidos: relaciones indígenas de la conquista.* 4th ed. Mexico City: UNAM, 1969.

Martínez, Carlos. *Tlatelolco: Tres instantáneas.* Mexico City: Editorial Jus, 1972.

Meyer, Michael C. and William L. Sherman. *The Course of Mexican History.* 3rd ed. New York: Oxford UP, 1987.

Miller, Beth, and Alfonso González. *26 Autoras del México Actual.* Mexico City: Costa-Amic, 1978.

Pedén, Margaret Sayers. *Out of the Volcano.* Washington: Smithsonian Institution Press, 1991.

Poniatowska, Elena. *Fuerte es el silencio.* Mexico City: Ediciones Era, 1980.

WORKS CITED

———. *La noche de Tlatelolco*. Mexico City: Ediciones Era, 1971.

———. *Massacre in Mexico*. Trans. Helen R. Lane. New York: Viking, 1971.

———. *Nada, nadie: Las voces del temblor*. Mexico City: Ediciones Era, 1988.

———. "A Question Mark Engraved on my Eyelids." *The Writer on Her Work*. Vol. 2. Ed. Janet Sternburg. New York: W. W. Norton, 1991. 82–96.

Steele, Cynthia. "La mediación en las obras documentales de Elena Poniatowska." *Mujer y literatura mexicana y chicana: Culturas en contacto*. Primer Coloquio Fronterizo, 22–24 Apr. 1987. 211–219.

———. "Entrevista: Elena Poniatowska." *Hispamérica* 18 (Aug.–Dec. 1989): 89–105.

PART TWO: ANGELES MASTRETTA

Booth, Wayne. "Distance and Point-of-View: An Essay in Classification." *The Theory of the Novel*. Ed. Phillip Stevick. New York: Free Press, 1967. 87–107.

Cohn, Dorrit. *Transparent Minds*. Princeton: Princeton UP, 1978.

Gold, Janet N. "*Arráncame la vida:* Textual Complicity and the Boundaries of Rebellion." *Chasqui: Revista de Literatura Latinoamericana* 17.2 (Nov. 1988): 35–40.

Guillermoprieto, Alma. "Report from Mexico: Serenading the Future." *New Yorker* 9 Nov. 1992: 96–103.

Heilbrun, Carolyn. *Toward a Recognition of Androgyny*. New York: Alfred A. Knopf, 1972.

———. *Writing a Woman's Life*. New York: W. W. Norton, 1988.

Hodge, Robert, and Gunther Kress. *Social Semiotics*. Ithaca: Cornell UP, 1988.

Lejeune, Philippe. "The Autobiographical Contract." *French Literary Theory Today, a Reader*. Ed. Tzvetan Todorov. Cambridge: Cambridge UP, 1982. 192–222.

Mastretta, Angeles. *Arráncame la vida*. Mexico City: Cal y Arena, 1990.

———. *Mexican Bolero*. Trans. Ann Wright. London: Viking, 1991.

———. "Puerto libre: Memoria y acantilado." *Nexos* 15.175 (July 1992): 19–20.

Miller, Jane. *Women Writing about Men*. New York: Pantheon, 1986.

Pansters, Wil. *Politics and Power in Puebla*. Amsterdam: CEDLA, 1990.

WORKS CITED

Pedén, Margaret Sayers. *Out of the Volcano*. Washington: Smithsonian Institution Press, 1991.

Robles, Martha. *La sombra fugitiva: Escritoras en la cultura nacional*. Vol. 2. Mexico City: Editorial Diana, 1989.

Romberg, Bertil. *Studies in the Narrative Technique of the First-Person Novel*. Stockholm: Almqvist & Wiksell, 1962.

Ronfeldt, David. *Atencingo: The Politics of Agrarian Struggle in a Mexican Ejido*. Stanford: Stanford UP, 1973.

Teichmann, Reinhard. "Angeles Mastretta." *De la onda en adelante*. Mexico City: Editorial Posada, 1987. 505–22.

REVIEWS OF *MEXICAN BOLERO*

Gomis, Anamari. "Ella encarnaba boleros." *Nexos* 91 (July 1985): 51–52.

López González, Aralia. "Dos Tendencias en la evolución de la narrativa contemporánea de escritoras mexicanas." *Mujer y Literatura mexicana y chicana: Culturas en contacto*. Vol. 2. Mexico City: Colegio de México, 1990. 21–24.

McMurray, George. "Two Mexican Feminist Writers." *Hispania* 73 (Dec. 1990): 1035–36.

Kirkus Reviews 58 (1 May 1990): 602.

Peralta, Braulio. "Mi novela es una historia, no un ensayo feminista: Angeles Mastretta." *La Jornada* 11 June 1985. (Mexico City).

Polk, James. "Mexico: Beyond the machismo." *Philadelphia Inquirer* 8 July 1990: 3-F.

See, Carolyn. "Woman's Coming of Age in Mexico." *Los Angeles Times* 23 July 1990: E8.

PART THREE: SILVIA MOLINA

Brushwood, John S. *La novela mexicana (1967–1982)*. Mexico City: Grijalbo, 1984.

DuPlessis, Rachel Blau. *Writing Beyond the Ending*. Bloomington: Indiana UP, 1985.

Fuentes, Carlos. *Cervantes y la crítica de la lectura*. Mexico City: Joaquín Mortiz, 1976.

Hite, Molly. *The Other Side of the Story*. Ithaca: Cornell UP, 1989.

Hodge, Robert, and Gunther Kress. *Social Semiotics*. Ithaca: Cornell UP, 1988.

Kingsolver, Barbara. *Animal Dreams*. New York: HarperCollins, 1990.

WORKS CITED

Molina, Silvia. *Campeche: Punta del ala del país*. Mexico City: Consejo Nacional para la Cultura y las Artes, 1991.

———. *Imagen de Héctor*. Mexico City: Cal y Arena, 1990.

———. *La familia vino del norte*. 2nd ed. Mexico City: Aguilar, León y Cal Editores, 1989.

———. "La mujer en mi escritura/The Woman in my writing." Mexico City: *Roommate* 5 (May 1990): 21–22.

Pilnyak, Boris. *The Tale of the Unextinguished Moon and Other Stories*. New York: Washington Square, 1967.

Poniatowska, Elena. "Dorotea junto a la ventana." *La jornada de los libros* 126 (13 June 1987): 1, 6. (Mexico City).

Teichmann, Reinhard. "Identidad e historia en Silvia Molina." *Mujer y literatura mexicana y chicana: culturas en contacto*. Ed. López González, Aralia, et al. Mexico City: Colegio de México, 1990. 121–125.

———. "Silvia Molina." *De la onda en adelante: conversaciones con 21 novelistas mexicanos*. Mexico City: Posada, 1987. 291–312.

Torres, Vicente Francisco. "Silvia Molina: entre la historia y la novela." *Esta narrativa mexicana: ensayos y entrevistas*. Mexico City: Universidad Autónoma Metropolitana, 1991. 149–59.

Reviews of Silvia Molina's Work

Bolívar, María Dolores. "*Ascensión Tun* en la tradición del discurso de la mujer en América Latina." *Nuevo Texto Crítico* 4, Año 2 (Segundo semestre 1989): 137–43.

Domínguez Michale, Christopher. "Silvia Molina y la nueva retórica femenina." *Proceso* 27 July 1987: 58–59. (Mexico City).

Gallareta Negrón, Miguel. "Silvia Molina: escritora por asalto." *Vogue* [Mexico] 9 June 1987: 68–70. (Mexico City).

Jorajuria, David. "Bibliomanía: *La familia vino del norte*, de Silvia Molina." *El Búho* 14 June 1987. (Mexico City).

Lesi Márquez, Almicar. "Silvia Molina entre los fragmentos del tiempo." *La plaza* 22 (June 1987): 3–5. (Mexico City).

Torres, Vicente Francisco. "Mis novelas no son históricas: Silvia Molina." *Uno más uno* 3 Aug. 1987: 7. (Mexico City).

PART FOUR: BRIANDA DOMECQ

Domecq, Brianda. *Bestiario doméstico*. Mexico City: Fondo de Cultura Económica, 1992.

WORKS CITED

———. *BD: De cuerpo entero.* Mexico City: Ediciones Corunda, 1991.
———. "Escribir para reinventarse: tarea de la mujer (1): Constantes en cuatro novelas." *Excélsior* 23 Feb. 1981: 3, Cultural Section. (Mexico City).
———. "Las escritoras en la década de los 80." *Fem* 14.85 (Jan. 1990): 7–9. (Mexico City).
———. *La insólita historia de la Santa de Cabora.* Mexico City: Planeta, 1990.
———. *Once días y algo más.* 1979. Mexico City: HARLA, 1991.
Estés, Clarissa Pinkola. *Women Who Run with the Wolves: Myths and Stories of the Wild Woman Archetype.* New York, Ballantine, 1992.
González, Mirta A. "La mujer y la literatura mexicana." *Siempre* 2034 (17 June 1992): 2–4, section "La Cultura en México." (Mexico City).
Suleiman, Susan Rubin. *Subversive Intent: Gender, Politics, and the Avant-Garde.* Cambridge: Harvard UP, 1990.

Reviews of Brianda Domecq's novels

Acevedo Escobedo, Antonio. "Las experiencias de Brianda Domecq." *El Universal* 4 July 1981 (Mexico City).
Bárcenas, Angel. "Novela de un secuestro." *El nacional* 13 Dec. 1979: 17. (Mexico City).
Brushwood, John. "Una escritora entre dos mundos." *El Universal* 20 July 1981: 24, section "Culturales." (Mexico City).
Morales, Miguel Angel. "Los días de Brianda Domecq." *Excélsior* 20 Jan. 1980: 14, section "Diorama de la Cultura." (Mexico City).
Munguía Espitia, Jorge. "La santa de los pobres." *Proceso* 17 Dec. 1990: 61–62. (Mexico City).
Peralta, Elda. "Libros: *Once días y algo más.*" *El Heraldo Cultural* 825 (6 Sept. 1981): 7.
Solana, Rafael. "Brianda Domecq: una novelista insólita." *Siempre* 2027 (29 Apr. 1992). (Mexico City).

SELECT BIBLIOGRAPHY

BOOKS BY ELENA PONIATOWSKA

¡Ay vida!, no me mereces. Mexico City: Joaquín Mortíz, 1985.
La casa en la tierra. Mexico City: Instituto Nacional Indigenista INI-Fonapas, 1980.
Los cuentos de Lilus Kikus. Xalapa, Mexico: Universidad Veracruzana, 1967.
Dear Diego. Trans. Katherine Silver. New York: Pantheon, 1986.
De noche vienes. Mexico City: Ediciones Era, 1991.
Domingo 7. Mexico City: Ediciones Océano, 1982.
La "Flor de Lis." Mexico City: Ediciones Era, 1988.
Gaby Brimmer. Mexico City: Editorial Grijalbo, 1979.
Hasta no verte, Jesús mío. Mexico City: Ediciones Era, 1969.
Lilus Kikus. Los Presentes (series). Mexico City: Ediciones Era, 1985.
Melés y Teleo, apuntes para una comedia. Panoramas 5 (1956): 135–299.
Mujeres de Juchitán. Mexico City: Editorial Toledo, 1988.
Pablo O'Higgins. With Gilbert Bosques. Mexico City: Fondo Editorial de la Plástica Mexicana, 1984.
Palabras cruzadas. Mexico City: Ediciones Era, 1961.
El primer primero de mayo. Mexico City: Centro de Estudios Históricos del Movimiento Obrero Mexicano, 1976.
Querido Diego, te abraza Quiela. Mexico City: Ediciones Era, 1990.
Tinísima. Mexico City: Ediciones Era, 1992.
Todo empezó el domingo. Mexico City: Fondo de Cultura Económica, 1963.
El último guajolote. Mexico City: Cultura/SEP, 1983.
The Voice of the Powerless. Sound recording in English. Washington: National Public Radio, 1984.

WORKS ABOUT/INCLUDING ELENA PONIATOWSKA

Agosín, Marjorie. "The Message: Elena Poniatowska." Landscapes of a new land: Fiction by Latin American Women. Buffalo, NY: White Pine, 1989.
Alegría, Fernando, ed. Nueva historia de la novela hispanoamericana. Hanover, NH: Ediciones del Norte, 1986. 426–28.

SELECT BIBLIOGRAPHY

Campobello, Nellie. "Introduction." *Cartucho and My Mother's Hands*. Austin: U of Texas P, 1988. xiv.

Castellanos, Rosario. Prologue by Elena Poniatowska. *Meditación en el umbral: Antología poética*. Ed. Julian Palley. Mexico City: Fondo de Cultura Económica, 1985.

Chevigny, Bell Gale. "The Transformation of Privilege in the Work of Elena Poniatowska." *Faith of a Woman Writer*. Ed. Alice Kessler-Harris and William McBrien. Westport, CT: Greenwood, 1988.

Conger, Amy. *Compañeras de México: women photograph women*. Riverside: University Art Gallery, U of California, Riverside, 1990.

Davis, Lisa. "An Invitation to Understanding among Poor Women of the Americas: *The Color Purple* and *Hasta no verte Jesús mío*." Ed. Bell Gale Chevigny and Gari Laguardia. *Reinventing the Americas: Comparative Studies of literature of the United States and Spanish America*. New York: Cambridge UP, 1986. 224–41.

De Llarena, Elena. *14 mujeres escriben cuentos*. Mexico City: Federación Editorial Mexicana, 1975.

Dever, Susan. "Elena Poniatowska: La crítica de una mujer." *Mujer y literatura mexicana y chicana, culturas en contacto*. Ed. Aralia López González et al. Mexico City: Coloquio Fronterizo. 22–24 Apr. 1988. 107–11.

Dimitriou, Agnes L. "Entrevista con Elena Poniatowska." *Letras femeninas* 16.1–2 (Spring–Fall 1990): 125–33.

Erro-Peralta, Nora and Caridad Silva-Nuñez. *Beyond the Border*. Pittsburgh: Cleis, 1991. 144–48.

Fernández Olmos, Margarite. "El género testimonial: Aproximaciones feministas." *Revista/Review Interamericana* 11.1 (Spring 1981): 69–75.

Flori, Mónica. "El mundo femenino de Marta Lynch y Elena Poniatowska." *Letras femeninas* 9.2 (1983): 23–30.

———. "Visions of Women: Symbolic Physical Portrayal as Social Commentary in the Short Fiction of Elena Poniatowska." *Third Woman* 2.2 (1984): 77–83.

Fontaine, Joffre de la, ed. *Diez cuentos mexicanos contemporáneos*. Xalapa: Universidad Veracruzana, 1967.

Foster, David William. "Latin American Documentary Narrative." *Publications of the Modern Language Association of America* 99.1 (Jan. 1984): 41–55.

Fox-Lockert, Lucía. "Elena Poniatowska: *Hasta no verte Jesús mío* (1969)."

SELECT BIBLIOGRAPHY

Women novelists of Spain and Spanish America. Metuchen, NJ: Scarecrow, 1979. 260–77.

Franco, Jean. *Plotting Women: Gender and Representation in Mexico.* New York: Columbia UP, 1989.

Friedman, Edward H. "The Marginated Narrator: *Hasta no verte Jesús mío* and the Eloquence of Repression." *The Antiheroine's Voice: Narrative Discourse and Transformations of the Picaresque.* Columbia: U of Missouri P, 1987. 170–87.

García Pinto, Magdalena. "Entrevista con Elena Poniatowska, octubre de 1983, en su casa de Coyoacán." *Historias íntimas: conversaciones con diez escritoras latinoamericanas.* Hanover, NH: Ediciones del Norte, May 1988. 175–98.

Gazarian-Gautier, Marie-Lise. "Elena Poniatowska." *Interviews with Latin American Writers.* Elmwood Park, IL: Dalkey Archive, 1989. 199–216.

Gertel, Zunilda. "La mujer y su discurso: conciencia y máscara." *Cambio social en México visto por autores contemporáneos.* Ed. José Anadón. West Bend: U of Notre Dame and Sociedad de Escritores de México, 1989. 45–59.

González, Patricia, et al. "Testimonios de una escritora: Elena Poniatowska en micrófono." *La sartén por el mango, encuentro de escritoras latinoamericanas.* Ediciones Huracán, 1985: 155–62.

Gutiérrez, Ana. "Presentación al lector mexicano." *Se necesita muchacha.* Mexico City: Fondo de Cultura Económica, 1983. 7–86.

Gyurko, Lanin A. "The Literary Response to Nonoalco-Tlatelolco." *Contemporary Latin American Culture: Unity and Diversity.* Center for Latin American Studies, Tempe, Arizona SU, 1984. 45–78.

Hancock, Joel. "Elena Poniatowska's *Hasta no verte Jesús mío:* The Remaking of the Image of Woman." *Hispania* 66.3 (Sept. 1983): 353–59.

Jaén, Didier T. "La neopicaresca en México: Elena Poniatowska y Luis Zapata." *Tinta* 1.5 (Spring 1987): 23–29.

Jaramillo Levi, Enrique. *El cuento erótico en México,* Editorial Diana, 1975.

Jorgensen, Beth E. "La intertextualidad en *La noche de Tlatelolco* de Elena Poniatowska." *Hispanic Journal* 10.2 (Spring 1989): 81–93.

———. "Texto e ideología en la obra de Elena Poniatowska." *Dissertation Abstracts International* 47.4 (Oct. 1986): 1344a.

SELECT BIBLIOGRAPHY

Kiddle, Mary Ellen. "The *Novela Testimonial* in Contemporary Mexican Literature." *Confluencia* 1.1 (Fall 1985): 82–89.

Kushigian, Julia A. "Transgresión de la autobiografía y el Bildungsroman en *Hasta no verte Jesús mío*." *Revista Iberoamericana* 53.140 (July–Sept. 1987): 667–77.

Leal, Luis. "Tlatelolco, Tlatelolco." *Denver Quarterly* 14.1 (1979): 3–13.

Lemaitre, Monique. "Jesusa Palancares y la dialéctica de la emancipación femenina." *Hispamérica: Revista de Literatura* 10.30 (Dec. 1981): 131–35.

Mendez-Faith, Teresa. "Entrevista con Elena Poniatowska." *Revista de Literatura Hispánica* 15 (Spring 1982): 54–60.

Mendez-Faith, Teresa, and Elizabeth Heinicke. "Translation of an Interview with Elena Poniatowska." Trans. Elizabeth Heinicke. *Atlantis* 9.2 (Spring 1984): 70–75.

Menton, Seymour. "Sin embargo: La nueva cuentista femenina en México." *Tinta* 1.5 (Spring 1987): 35–37.

Miller, Beth Kurti. "Elena Poniatowska." *Mujeres en la literatura*. 2nd ed. Toluca: Universidad Autónoma del Estado de México, 1982. 89–91.

———. "Personajes y personas: Castellanos, Fuentes, Poniatowska y Saenz." *Mujeres en la literatura*. Toluca: Universidad Autónoma del Estado de México, 1982. 65–75.

———. "Elena Poniatowska." *Latin American Literary Review* 4.7 (1975): 73–78.

———. "Interview with Elena Poniatowska." *Latin American Literary Review* 4.7 (1975): 73–78.

Minc, S. Rose, and Marilyn R. Frankenthaler, eds. *Requiem for the Boom—Premature?: A Symposium*. Upper Montclair, NJ: Montclair State College, 1980.

Ocampo, Aurora M. *Cuentistas Mexicanas Siglo XX*. Mexico City: Universidad Nacional Autónoma de México, 1976.

Poot-Herrera, Sara. "La 'Flor de Lis,' códice y huella de Elena Poniatowska." *Mujer y literatura mexicana y chicana: Culturas en contacto II*. Ed. Aralia López González, et al. Mexico City: Colegio de Mexico, 1990.

Poniatowska, Elena. "And Here's to You, Jesusa." Trans. Gregory Kolovakos and Ronald Christ. *Lives on the Line: The Testimony of Contemporary Latin American Authors*. Ed. Doris Meyer. Berkeley: U of California P, 1988.

SELECT BIBLIOGRAPHY

Portal, Marta. *Proceso narrativo de la revolución mexicana*. Madrid: Espasa-Calpe, 1980. 285–92.

Radchik, Laura. "Las memorias de Cronos en las manecillas de Dios." *Plural* (cultural supplement of *Excélsior*) 204 (Sept. 1988): 82–85.

Resnick, Margery, and Isabelle de Courtivron. *Women Writers in Translation: An Annotated Bibliography 1945–1982*. New York: Garland, 1984. 243.

Richards, Katherine. "A Note on Contrasts in Elena Poniatowska's *De noche vienes*." *Letras femeninas* 17 (Spring–Fall 1991): 1–2, 107–111.

Roses, Lorraine. "Entrevista con Elena Poniatowska." *Plaza* 5–6 (Fall–Spring 1981–82): 51–64.

Sefchovich, Sara. "Elena." *Nexos* 13.151 (July 1990): 10–11.

Shea, Maureen Elizabeth. *Latin American Women Writers and the Growing Potential of Political Consciousness*. Dissertation Abstracts International, Ann Arbor, MI. Sept. 1988. 49:3, 515A.

———. "A Growing Awareness of Sexual Oppression in the Novels of Contemporary Latin American Women Writers." *Confluencia* 4.1 (Fall 1988): 53–59.

Smith, Kim L. *Silence in Four Works of Elena Poniatowska: A Socioliterary Approach*. Dissertation Abstracts International. Vol 50, No. 2. Aug 1989. 454A.

Starcevic, Elizabeth. "Breaking the Silence: Elena Poniatowska, A Writer in Transition." *Literatures in Transition: The Many Voices of the Carribbean Area: A Symposium*. Gaithersburg, MD; Upper Montclair, NJ: Hispamérica, 1982.

———. "Elena Poniatowska: Witness for the people." *Contemporary Women Authors of Latin America: Introductory Essays*. Ed. Doris Meyer and Margarite Fernandez Olmos. Brooklyn: Brooklyn College P, 1983. viii, 101.

———. "Neglected by the Boom: So What Else is New?" *Requiem for the Boom—Premature: A Symposium*. Ed. Rose S. Minc and Marilyn R. Frankenthaler. Montclair, NJ: Montclair State College, 1980: 103–9.

Steele, Cynthia. "La Creatividad y el deseo en *Querido Diego, te abraza Quiela* de Elena Poniatowska." *Hispamérica* 14.41 (Aug. 1985): 17–28.

Tatum, Charles M. "Elena Poniatowska's *Hasta no verte Jesús mío*."

SELECT BIBLIOGRAPHY

Latin American women writers: yesterday and today. Pittsburgh: Latin American Literary Review, 1977. 49–58.

Taylor, Kathleen, and Deborah Wilson. *La nueva narrativa mexicana: Revisiones y subversiones de la historia*. Dissertation Abstracts International, Ann Arbor, MI. Oct, 1989. 50:4, 959A.

Young, Dolly J. "Mexican Literary Reactions to Tlatelolco 1968." *Latin American Research Review* 20.2 (1985): 71–85.

Young, Dolly J, and William D Young. "The New Journalism in Mexico: Two Women Writers." *Chasqui: Revista de Literatura Latinoamericana* 12.2–3 (Feb.–May 1983): 72–80.

BOOKS BY ANGELES MASTRETTA

Mujeres de ojos grandes. Barcelona: Seix Barral, 1991.
La pájara pinta. New York: Macmillan, 1987.

WORKS ABOUT/INCLUDING MASTRETTA

Anderson, Danny J. "Displacement: Strategies of Transformation in *Arráncame la vida*." *Journal of the Midwest Modern Language Association* 21.1 (Spring 1988): 15–27.

Beer, Gabriela de. "Entre la aventura y el litigio: Una entrevista con Angeles Mastretta." *Nexos* 184 (Apr. 1993): 33–39.

WORKS BY SILVIA MOLINA

El algodón. Mexico City: Editorial Patria, 1990.
Ascensión Tun. Mexico City: Martín Casillas Editores, 1981.
A vuelta de correo. Prologue by Alfonso Reyes. Mexico City: Universidad Autónoma de México, 1988.
Los cuatro hermanos. Mexico City: Ediciones Corunda, 1988.
Dicen que me case yo. Mexico City: Ediciones Cal y Arena, 1991.
Gray Skies Tomorrow. Trans. John Mitchell and Ruth Mitchell de Aguilar. Kaneohe, HI: Plover, 1993.
Un hombre cerca. Mexico City: Cal y Arena, 1992.
El hombre equivocado. Mexico City: Joaquín Mortíz, 1988. (Novel by eleven authors.)
La leyenda del sol y de la luna. Mexico City: Trillas, 1992.
Leyendo en la tortuga. Mexico City: Martín Casillas Editores, 1981.

SELECT BIBLIOGRAPHY

Lides de estaño. Mexico City: Universidad Autónoma Metropolitana, 1984.
El papel. Mexico City: Editorial Patria, 1985.

WORKS ABOUT/INCLUDING SILVIA MOLINA

Medina, Manuel F. *La búsqueda de la autoidentidad en las novelas históricas de Silvia Molina.* M.A. thesis. Dept. of Spanish and Portuguese, Brigham Young U, Aug. 1990.

Morales, Mariano, ed. "Promoción y difusión de la literatura joven en México." *Por la literatura! Mujeres y escritura en México.* Puebla: Universidad Autónoma de Puebla, 1992. 122–25.

Pedén, Margaret Sayers. "Literature." *Latin American Literary Review* 19 (Jan./June 1991): 123–25.

Samperio, Guillermo. *Miedo ambiente y otros miedos.* Mexico City: Secretaría de Ed. Pública (SEP), 1986.

BOOKS BY BRIANDA DOMECQ

Acechando al unicornio. Mexico City: Fondo de Cultura Económica, 1988.
Mujer que publica, mujer pública. Mexico City: Diana, forthcoming.
Voces y rostros del Bravo. Mexico City: Editorial Jilguero, 1987.

STORIES IN ENGLISH BY BRIANDA DOMECQ

"Bitter Autumn." *Marriage* 8.50 (Aug. 1968): 62–67.
"Adelaide's Body." Trans. Carolyn Brushwood. *River Styx* 26 (1988): 80–82. St. Louis: Missouri Arts Council.
"The Eternal Theater." Trans. Carolyn Brushwood. *Latin American Literary Review* 19.38 (July–Dec. 1991): 96–99.

WORKS ABOUT/INCLUDING BRIANDA DOMECQ

López González, Aralia. "La huella de lo reprimido: fisuras y suturas." *Signos: Anuario de humanidades* 5.1 (1991): 239–48.

GENERAL REFERENCE AND LITERARY THEORY

Abel, Elizabeth, ed. *Writing and Sexual Difference.* Chicago: U of Chicago P, 1982.

Bassnett, Susan, ed. *Knives and Angels: Women Writers in Latin America.* London: Zed, 1990.

Brushwood, John S. *La novela mexicana (1967–1982).* Mexico City: Grijalbo, 1985.

SELECT BIBLIOGRAPHY

Camp, Roderic A. *Intellectuals and the State in Twentieth-Century Mexico.* Austin: U of Texas P, 1985.

Cortina, Lynn Ellen Rice. *Spanish-American Women Writers—A Bibliography Research Checklist.* New York: Garland, 1983.

Ecker, Gisela. *Estética feminista.* Barcelona: Icaria, 1986.

Eco, Umberto. *Tratado de semiótica general.* Trans. Carlos Manzano. Barcelona: Editorial Lumen, 1981.

Fox-Lockert, Lucía. *Women Novelists in Spain and Spanish America.* Metuchen, NJ: Scarecrow, 1979.

Franco, Jean. *Plotting Women: Gender and Representation in Mexico.* New York: Columbia UP, 1989.

Fuentes, Carlos. *Cervantes o la crítica de la lectura.* Mexico City: Editorial Joaquín Mortiz, 1976.

Kaminsky, Amy. *Reading the Body Politic: Feminist Criticism and Latin American Women Writers.* Minneapolis: U of Minnesota P, 1992.

Leal, Luis. "Female Archetypes in Mexican Literature." *Women in Hispanic Literature: Icons and Fallen Idols.* Ed. Beth Miller. Berkeley: U of California P, 1983. 227–42.

Magnarelli, Sharon. *The Lost Rib: Female Characters in the Spanish-American Novel.* Lewisburg, PA: Bucknell UP, 1985.

Miller, Beth, ed. *Women in Hispanic Literature.* Berkeley: U of California P, 1983.

Morales, Mariano, ed. *Por la literatura! Mujeres y escritura en México.* Puebla: Universidad Autónoma de Puebla, 1992.

Pacheco, José Emilio. "Crónica de Huitzilac." *La sombra de serrano selecciones.* Mexico City: SEP, 1989. 13–31.

Pratt, Annis. *Archetypal Patterns in Women's Fiction.* Bloomington: Indiana UP, 1981.

Robles, Martha. "Elena Poniatowska." *La sombra fugitiva: Escritoras en la cultura nacional.* Mexico City: Universidad Nacional Autónoma de México, 1985. 343–65.

Schaefer, Claudia. *Textured Lives: Women, Art, and Representation in Modern Mexico.* Tucson: U of Arizona P, 1992.

Secanella, Petra M. *El periodismo político en México.* Barcelona: Editorial Mitre, 1983.

Showalter, Elaine, ed. *The New Feminist Criticism.* New York: Pantheon, 1985.

Silverman, Kaja. *The Subject of Semiotics.* New York: Oxford UP, 1983.

SELECT BIBLIOGRAPHY

Steele, Cynthia. *Beyond the Pyramid: Politics, Gender and The Mexican Novel, 1968–1988*. Austin: U of Texas P, 1992.

Valis, Noel, and Carol Maier, eds. *In the Feminine Mode: Essays on Hispanic Women Writers*. Lewisburg, PA: Bucknell UP, 1990.

Vanderwood, Paul. "La santa batalla de la niña de Cabora." *La Jornada Semanal* 23 (July 1991): 34–40.

Welles, Marcia L. "The Changing Face of Women in Latin American Fiction." *Women in Hispanic Literature: Icons and Fallen Idols*. Berkeley: U of California P, 1983. 280–88.